LOVE, HONOR, AND VIRTUE

Gaining or Re-Gaining a Biblical Attitude Toward Sexuality

Hal & Melanie Young

GREAT WATERS PRESS
MAKING BIBLICAL FAMILY LIFE PRACTICAL

Love, Honor, and Virtue

First edition, February 2017.

Publisher's Cataloging-in-Publication Data

Young, Hal, 1964-
    Love, honor, and virtue: gaining or re-gaining a biblical attitude toward sexuality / Hal and Melanie Young
       88 p. 23cm.
       ISBN 978-1-938554-12-4 (pbk.)
       1. Young Men—Religious Life. 2. Chastity. 3. Sex—Religious Aspects—Christianity. I. Young, Melanie, 1964-. II. Title.
       BV4541.3.Y68
       241.66

DEDICATION

TO ROGER AND JAN SMITH

We met Roger and Jan Smith as fellow leaders in the Christian homeschooling movement. We began as colleagues but rapidly became friends, and their open hearts, shared wisdom, and gracious hospitality have been an encouragement and example to us, time and again. They have touched us like they touch so many, and our family is richer because of it!

When we were struggling to find time and focus to finish this book, they scooped up the whole family of Youngs, planted the parents in a quiet cabin, and gave the children a country vacation they've talked about endlessly. Whenever we talk about travel plans, one child will invariably ask, "Will we see the Smiths?"

For their inspiration and support at that critical moment, we'd like to dedicate this project to Dr. Roger Smith, M.D., and his wife and best friend, Jan Smith, who make northern Louisiana a special place in all our hearts.

CONTENTS

Introduction

To the Young Men on the Battlefield

One of the sobering truths of military history is that an army tends to approach each war with the weapons and tactics of the last one. It's a tough start that can turn to disaster if the army doesn't learn and adapt quickly.

In 1755, when the red-coated British Regulars marched into the American wilderness to confront the French and their Iroquois allies, they expected to dominate the battlefield with disciplined maneuvers, volleys of musket fire, and relentless advances with fixed bayonets. That's what won battles in Europe.

But those tactics didn't work for fighting Indians.

It was pointless to protest, as some did, that Indian tactics were beneath the honor of a gentleman soldier. Sheltering behind rocks and trees, shooting the officers from their horses and melting into the forest—why wouldn't they stand and fight *properly?*

The answer, of course, is the British had to learn what soldiers have learned again and again over the centuries: you have to fight the war you *have*, not the war you *want* to have.

There's a war going on for the souls of men, and for the souls of young men in particular.

1

The hottest part of that battle is likely the matter of sexual purity. Many of the older soldiers don't realize how the fight has changed. They remember engaging the battle years ago and learning to combat the enemy's weapons and ambushes for that time. With God's help, they may have learned how to detect the hidden traps as new threats were deployed. Maybe the enemy shifted his focus to attack them in different areas.

But you're in the thick of that fight right now, and you need all the help you can get. That's the reason for this book.

Who do we have in mind as our readers? We are aiming for you, men and young men, who are struggling with the temptations and challenges of bachelorhood. We know it's not easy. The world is throwing itself at you in a way we haven't seen since the days of the Roman Empire.

And guys are being drawn into the fight younger and younger. When we first started writing and teaching on this issue just a few years ago, we heard from parents whose 17- or 16-year-old sons were having trouble with temptations—typically relating to pornography. It has rapidly moved to worries over 12-year-olds, 10-year-olds, even boys 8 and under.

So if you're in your teens or twenties and feeling like there are temptations and pressures coming at you faster than you can process, you're not imagining it. We'll talk more about why that fact is, but for now, understand that even if you're on the younger end of that range, the battle is real and personal for you, too.

Where We're Coming From

We write from a Christian perspective. Even if you don't share our worldview, there are good secular reasons to keep sexuality within the boundary of marriage, and we will talk about some of these in the pages ahead. But we believe the Bible is God's word and serves as a reliable guidebook for life, faith, and relationships, even in 21st Century America. We don't apologize for that, we just want you to know where we come from. We're not psychologists or therapists, but a couple with a healthy marriage, six sons and two daughters, a lot of experience, and a lot of time studying the Bible and trying to put it into practice in our family life. We are going to speak frankly about topics we'd rather avoid, because we want you to be encouraged and equipped for life in a challenging world.

That world is coming for you and you need to be ready to engage the battle when it arrives. Avoiding it is not an option. You're either a warrior, or a victim. We want to help you meet the challenge with your weapons ready.

And we ought to say that in our home, we consider anyone over the age of 13 as a young man, not a boy.

Here's why. In the Bible, there seem to be two stages of life—childhood and adulthood. The apostle Paul, writing to the church in Corinth, said, *When I was a child, I spoke as a child, I understood as a child, I thought as a child; but when I became a man, I put away childish things.* [1] Notice he doesn't mention a middle stage we call adolescence or the teen years. Apparently, there's one, and then the other—either a child, or a man.

The Bible does talk about youth. There is definitely a stage of early adulthood in which young guys still need training, supervision, and mentoring. But look at the passages which describe "youth" and ask yourself, does this sound like the teen group at church?

When David confronted Goliath, he was warned that the giant had been a man of war *from his youth.* [2]

When God called the prophet Jeremiah, he protested, *Behold, I cannot speak, for I am a youth,* and God responded, *Do not say, 'I am a youth.' For you shall go to all to whom I send you, And whatever I command you, you shall speak.* [3]

Paul wrote to Timothy and advised him, *Let no one despise your youth* (another translation says, *Let no one look down on your youthfulness*), *but be an example to the believers...* [4] Timothy had been traveling with Paul in his missionary work, and Paul left him behind to continue the work in Ephesus while the apostle went on to Macedonia.

---

1 1 Corinthians 13:11

2 1 Samuel 17:33

3 Jeremiah 1:6-7

4 1 Timothy 4:12

Other passages describe youths as husbands and fathers—*Rejoice with the wife of your youth*[5]and *Like arrows in the hand of a warrior, So are the children of one's youth,*[6] for examples.

So yes, there is such a thing as youth in the Bible. They are young men who have doubts, fears, and lack of experience, but they are also husbands, fathers, missionaries, prophets, and warriors. They're young, but they're not kids.

And youths are capable of quite adult sins. God observes that *the imagination of man's heart is evil from his youth,*[7] Job complains that God will *make me inherit the iniquities of my youth,*[8] the psalmist prays to God, *Do not remember the sins of my youth,*[9] and God tells the prophet Jeremiah, *the children of Israel and the children of Judah have done only evil before Me from their youth.*[10] So, when it comes to sexuality, we've got to recognize that you young men are *men*—and are facing temptations toward very serious sins. We know these are real issues for you. Since we began talking with parents about this subject, we've heard time and time again from young men who fell into sexual immorality when they were 12 or 13 and spent years secretly fighting, and falling, and falling again, into the same sexual sins...and others.

So, for all of you, we want to help you fight this battle—to win!

A Note to the Church and Families at Large

Several years ago, we began speaking and writing about raising sons. We quickly discovered a large discrepancy between the reality of boys' developing sexuality and the way parents were thinking and talking about it. Most of the teaching resources on the subject seemed to be written for the parents of girls. The problem is our daughters' timetables are different, their sensitivities and attractions are different, and from our observation, the advice we might give our daughters was inadequate counsel given too late for our sons.

---

5 Proverbs 5:18

6 Psalm 127:4

7 Genesis 8:21

8 Job 13:26

9 Psalm 25:7

10 Jeremiah 32:30

We actually meet parents who ask, "Can't we just have a talk about this subject the week before our son gets married?" We hear from mothers who are embarrassed and angry that their husbands or church leaders think these matters should be discussed with pre-teens as well as older sons. We find parents, who believed they had total control over their sons' media, shocked to discover how easily pornography can be accessed without a credit card and how casually friends will share those images on their phones or tablets.

So we began speaking and writing on this subject in hopes of helping parents with sons to understand their needs and how they differ from the needs of their daughters. Most of our message has been aimed at parents, but we were often asked, "What would you recommend as a resource to use with our sons?" We were also encouraged by young men to consider writing on the subject *for them,* which is the point of this book.

However, we want to encourage parents, church leaders, and others who may give this book to young men, to see it as a tool and not "the answer." This book can spark a long and productive series of conversations about sexuality, purity, sin and forgiveness, relationships, and other topics—and we think it's best used in that context.

1

SEX WAS GOD'S IDEA

It Started in the Garden

At some time, every coach in every sport will say "It's time to work on fundamentals." The Bible says something similar in the book of Psalms: *"If the foundations are destroyed, what can the righteous do?"*[1] Whenever we consider a big, complex subject full of moving parts, it's good to start at the beginning.

The God who made us didn't leave us alone to fumble around and try to invent a way of understanding life; He gave us guidance, if we're willing to look at it. Too often, we aren't. We men are famous for ignoring road maps, skipping over the owner's manual, and trusting our own ability to figure things out. Don't stay up late waiting for us to stop and ask for directions, either. Don't they punch your man card or something if you admit you're lost? If we're honest, most men can tell you stories of expensive mistakes, costly errors, and painful results from that kind of thinking.

If we want to succeed in the confusing world of relationships and sexuality, if we want to honor God with all our heart, mind, and strength, then we have to consider what the Maker told us about the system He created. We need to go back to the foundations and work on the fundamentals. What has God told us about His design and purpose for our sexuality? What should virtue look like?

---

1 Psalm 11:3

Where Do We Start?

The original design is laid out in the very first chapters of Genesis. Why go all the way back there? Because Genesis 1 and 2 describe the world as God originally created it, without sin, corruption, decay, or deformity. It was perfect as God delivered it.

The Creation is also the common past we share with all of humanity. The lessons we draw from Genesis 1-2—one theologian named them "Creation mandates"—apply to every person.[2] They were put in place before there were nations, religions, or cultures. They're not the social preferences of people who call themselves Christian, but belong to every kingdom and tribe in history. In later times, God gave directions specifically to Jews, or to Gentile nations, or to the early church and the generations of believers which followed. In the very beginning, though, He gave directions for all of mankind.

It's also worth noting that when Jesus taught about marriage, He went back to Genesis,[3] as did the apostle Paul.[4] There, and in other places, they spoke of the Genesis record as historical fact, not as an illustration or an allegory. If they took it seriously, then we should, too.

Sex and Gender Are God's Original Design

This morning we were reading a story about someone who said she was a woman and looked like a woman, but when she went through the airport scanner, the scanner which was programmed for a woman's body, saw an anomaly. The security agents responded immediately. No, there was no bomb, the "woman" had male parts! They told this passenger to go back through the scanner with it programmed for a man's body, but he refused. He insisted he was a woman.

We live in a time of discussion and confusion about gender, but God's design is straightforward: He created two humans in two genders which are central to fulfilling His purpose in creating them. In Genesis 1 we read:

---

2 It was John Murray in his book, *Principles of Conduct,* if you're interested.

3 See Matthew 19:3-6 and Mark 10:2-9, where Jesus refers to Genesis 1:27-28 and 2:24 to answer questions about marriage and divorce.

4 Paul uses Genesis 2:24 teaching on the nature of marriage in Ephesians 5:22-33.

God created man in His own image; in the image of God He created him; male and female He created them. Then God blessed them, and God said to them, "Be fruitful and multiply; fill the earth and subdue it ..."[5]

That tells us several serious foundational facts. First, God designed us from the very start to be male or female. Man and Woman together tell us something about the nature of God. With all of their differences, they are both created in His image, to illustrate and imitate God's character in some way. Appreciating all of their distinctive characteristics helps us understand God Himself.

Second, our sexuality, our maleness and femaleness, is a created design feature, not a choice to make later. In fact, the repeating phrases, *"God created man ... He created him ... He created them,"* are a classic form of emphasis in the original Hebrew language of the Old Testament. God made us, by His own design, for His own purposes. He doesn't give us the task of discovering or defining our gender; the Creator *creates* us as one or the other; *male and female He created them.*

The passage also tells us that God created the sexual act and told the very first humans to use it. How else could they populate the world and fill it with more human beings?

Our sexual distinctions are a crucial part of God's design for humanity and part of how He reveals Himself to mankind. There is a purpose for our being male or female!

God Created Marriage for Many Purposes

When you read the whole account of Creation in Genesis 1 and 2, you'll notice that God announces His satisfaction with each step of the process. He created light and pronounced it good; He defined the seas and dry land and pronounced *them* good; He created the plant kingdom, established the stars and planets in the heavens, and filled the earth with fish and birds and land animals of all sorts—and each time, God saw that *it was good* (Genesis 1:4, 10, 12, 18, 21, and 25).

When He created the first man, though, He points out a difference. "It is *not good,*" God said, *"that man should be alone."* He doesn't stop there—He announces

5 Genesis 1:27-28

His concluding act: *"I will make him a helper comparable to him."*[6] When He had made the Woman who corresponds to the Man, only then did God approve—and He underlined it: *Then God saw everything that He had made, and indeed it was very good.*[7]

What difference does that make? To begin with, we have to understand that creating the first woman was not Plan B. God didn't create Adam, step back from His work, and muse, "Hmm … that's not quite right." Sometimes Melanie looks into the boys' room with the stinky socks and sweaty, dirty boy-smell and teases them, "You need a help meet!" God announces this fact to go on record, though: Men, as a rule, are not meant to go through life alone. God created women to be our complement, the other side of God's image. It is part of God's design that we should look at Woman and see her as desirable—a helper, companion, and friend who meets needs we can't supply by ourselves.

We can also see that marriage between one man and one woman is part of God's original plan. The family is not a cultural norm which was adopted because it was a useful social structure. It wasn't a patch for a faulty creation or a fallen world later. God's design for humanity is wrapped up in marriage between opposite sexes. It's the assumed plan for nearly all of us. (The rest are called to celibacy, which we'll talk about later).

In Genesis, we can see three clear purposes for marriage. God created Woman to alleviate Man's loneliness; they were meant to be friends. She was made to be his helper; they have a mission and work to do on earth, and they need one another to bring it all about. And in fulfilling the Creation mandate to "fill the earth," she was meant to be his sexual partner for conceiving and bringing children into the world.

The New Testament takes it further. Genesis tells us that Man and Woman, together, give an illustration of the rich character of God, who is both mighty and merciful, for one example. When the apostle Paul wrote to the church he founded in Ephesus, he went to the next step and explained the relationship between a husband and wife is meant to be a picture of the way Jesus loves and provides for His people (in other words, the church), and the way the church

---

6 Genesis 2:18

7 Genesis 1:31

loves and honors Jesus.[8] When we do marriage right, we're living pictures of Jesus and *His* bride. That's pretty amazing!

But Paul also points out that, in our fallen world, marriage now has an important role in preventing sin. The ancient city of Corinth was famous for sexual immorality—the Greeks even had an idiom, "to act like a Corinthian," which was a polite way of describing someone whose lifestyle was in the gutter. When Paul founded a church there, new believers, trying to shake off the temptations and guilt of their former lives, asked if they should just swear off sex and friendships with women altogether. No, Paul wrote; since they were surrounded by sensual temptation, they should get married instead. *"[Because] of sexual immorality,"* he wrote, *"let each man have his own wife, and let each woman have her own husband. ... For it is better to marry than to burn* with passion."[9]

Our own society is much like the one surrounding the Corinthian church—highly sexualized and flooded with temptations. What the Bible tells us is that if we have sexual desires and longings, they are meant to be satisfied with our spouses, not by any other substitute—not by another woman or man, an object, a fantasy, or anything else. *There are immoralities all around us,* Paul is saying, *and God's provision for those passions is found in marriage.*

It's good to realize that God created our sexual natures and blessed them, too. He understands that we feel desire and temptation in those areas and instead of saying we have to ignore them or deny they exist, He provides clear guidelines and guardrails which allow us to enjoy this gift without guilt or shame. We can even expect joy, fun, and happiness there. There are times and situations when we have to double our guard or even run from temptation, but it's not forever and always.

For a young, unmarried man, though, there is a battle to fight—and win. God provided marriage as our safe harbor for sexual desire and expression, and told us, "He who *finds a wife, finds a good* thing..."[10]—but until we find that wife, we have to figure out how to live a life of virtue and self-control. It's a fight for a strong man, it will take some spiritual muscle, and we're going to talk about how you can become that valiant hero.

---

8 Ephesians 5:22-33

9 1 Corinthians 7:2,9

10 Proverbs 18:22

Summary

- God created our sexuality and He made us one of two genders as part of His original design

- Our sexuality is part of our purpose in life, and God blesses it to carry out His plans for individuals and all of mankind

- God created marriage for many purposes, including sexual expression and enjoyment

- All of us are expected to reserve our passion for our spouse alone

2

IT'S ALL CONNECTED

Marriage Education, Not Sex Education

Did anyone ever have "The Talk" with you? You know the one, where they blush and stare over your shoulder or down at the floor while they talk around the idea of sexuality and then say, "So, do you have any questions?".

Hopefully, you had parents or a mentor that didn't just have "the talk", but had many conversations about this topic with you throughout your childhood and young adulthood. Someone that really did answer your questions, even the ones you were afraid to ask. Someone who put it all into Biblical context. Someone who didn't just warn you of the dangers, but told you that God created sex and that it was very good within marriage.

But since most of us didn't have someone to do that for us, we're going to take some time to talk about the biology of it all. Now, you may be thinking, "Hey, I know all that stuff. I, uh, well, I've pretty much seen it all online." Even if you think you've seen everything there is to see, that doesn't mean you know how it works, or even what it's supposed to be like. So, let's talk.

Male and Female

We talked in the last chapter about how God created humans as male and female. From the moment of conception, when the DNA, or genes, of the sperm and egg unite, that new creation is either male, with an X and a Y chromosome, or female, with two X chromosomes. So, we are sexually differentiated from the beginning—one of two genders, male or female. Even within the womb, testosterone and estrogen are produced, male and female organs begin to form, and even brain development is different for the two genders.

If you've been wondering, "Am I a girl trapped in a guy's body?" we would say no. Based on the Word of God and seconded by science, you are either male or female. You might be a compassionate, gentle, nurturing kind of guy and that's okay. You might be tempted to certain kinds of sins that make you question your gender. But being tempted by sin isn't the same as sinning, and even if you do sin, it doesn't change who you are, genetically. Keep reading, we'll talk more about this later.

Boys and Girls

Even before puberty, boys and girls are different. Boys and girls process language differently.[1] They even hear differently: Girls are more sensitive to the sound of the human voice, while boys can handle a higher level of background noise than girls can. They usually play differently.

Now, we're not saying that it's not normal for a girl to want to play with trucks or a boy to pick up a doll and play. Sure, they do those things! But, they usually have different ways of playing with those things and play with them for different reasons. We have to remember, too, that a range of personalities is normal. Some girls are adventurous and some boys are timid, but they are still girls and boys.

Boys Becoming Men

There comes a time when a couple of genes that have been lying dormant begin to notify the hypothalamus (an area of the brain) to release GnRH, gonadotropin-releasing hormone. That's a $10 word, but it's not that hard to understand. Gonad means sex gland and -tropin comes from –tropic which means to change or mature in a specific way. So GnRH means a hormone that causes sex organ-maturing hormones to be released. That hormone stimulates the pituitary, a very important gland near your brain that is only the size of a

---

1 Northwestern University. "Boys' And Girls' Brains Are Different: Gender Differences In Language Appear Biological." ScienceDaily. ScienceDaily, 5 March 2008. <www.sciencedaily.com/releases/2008/03/080303120346.htm>.

pea, to release hormones that make boys' testes produce testosterone and girls' ovaries to produce estrogen. It sounds complicated—and it is, but it is also fascinating to understand the complexity of God's creation.

Once these hormones are flowing, changes start happening. The first changes, oddly enough, are emotional. Guys going through this tend to alternate between anger and rage and sadness and feeling depressed. We're used to thinking of adult women as hormonal, but guys get hormonal too! And most of them don't realize that's what's going on. They feel angry. Whenever they felt angry before, someone had been ugly to them or there was a conflict, so they start looking around for someone to be mad at or a conflict to engage in. Not good.

It doesn't help that our enemy, the devil, seems to be whispering in their ears, "They don't like you. Your parents don't really care about you. Nobody cares about you." It's a lie, but it's pretty believable when your emotions are going crazy in a way they never have before.

There are mental changes too. Kids this age begin to be able to think logically, to make connections between things they've learned in different subjects, and to begin to analyze facts and come to some conclusions. By the time they're 12 or 13, they'll be learning to think more abstractly. That's why you can't usually teach algebra to the smartest 7-year-old—they just aren't developmentally ready to understand it.

These emotional and mental changes tend to lead to spiritual doubts. The child who just "loved Jesus" becomes the preteen who is wondering if God is real. This can cause some panic for those kids (and their parents—ask us how we know!). It's not altogether a bad thing, though. This is the time a young man can make his faith his own. He just needs to ask those questions, seek out the truth, and realize that Christianity can stand up to his examination. If you're at that place, find someone who can give you answers, or even go find them yourself.[2]

We start seeing physical changes, too, of course (See, we're getting there. Be patient, we're going to talk about sex in a minute.) The first changes we noticed in our boys were kind of subtle. We saw their shoulders widening, their jaws

---

2 Got spiritual doubts? Wondering if Christianity is really true? These books helped us a lot: *Mere Christianity* by C.S. Lewis, *More Than a Carpenter* and *The New Evidence That Demands a Verdict* by Josh McDowell, and *The Case for Christ* by Lee Strobel.

strengthening, and they began to stink. Wait, never mind, that last part wasn't subtle at all. Sometimes they get chubby before their growth spurt starts. Often, their breasts swell some, which can pretty alarming to a boy, but it's natural and will go away on its own. Also, pubic hair growth starts and their genitals grow larger.

Behind the scenes, changes are happening in the testicles or testes, the two egg-shaped organs that hang in the scrotum behind the penis. Some cells are busy producing testosterone and other hormones, while other cells start their journey to becoming sperm. They will divide and develop until the sperm, a cell containing one set of chromosomes (normal cells contain two) and a long tail to propel it to its destination, is complete. Many millions are developing at a time.

Sometime in this transitional time, boys will start growing like crazy. Sometimes they grow 4 or 5 inches or more in a year! Different parts of the body grow at different rates, so they may be awkward for a while, but it will all even up in the end. Eventually, young men will grow hair in their armpits and on their faces, and the hair on the rest of their body will coarsen and thicken, especially on the chest.

Finally, the time will come when the system works and ejaculation occurs. Ejaculation is the release of semen through the penis. Semen is sperm (millions at a time) and the fluid around the sperm. For many young men, that happens in sleep. It's called nocturnal emission, or a wet dream. Sometimes those dreams are sexual in nature, but they're just as likely to be weird dreams of swimming or going to the bathroom. It can be pretty embarrassing to wake up with your underwear and sometimes sheets all sticky, but there's no reason at all to be ashamed. This is the normal and natural way God provided for the sperm that is being produced to be released without sin when a man's not married. Just strip the bed and wash your sheets if you need to.

Other changes are going on, too. We all know a guy's voice will start cracking, become unreliable, and finally deepen in tone, to his relief. He'll build more muscle mass and grow in strength. Young men also often grow intellectually and have an interest in learning more. Guys usually hit their stride academically when they get to high school and college.

Girls Becoming Women

Meanwhile, similar things are going on in the girls. Breast development usually comes first, but she'll soon see pubic hair and a couple of years later, underarm hair. Just like boys, girls usually have to go through a time of chubbiness before they start growing in height and become shapelier as their hips widen and breasts grow.

On the inside, her ovaries, small glands near her uterus, or womb, start producing estrogen and other hormones. Eggs inside her ovary begin to mature and her uterus and vagina, the passage between her uterus and the outside, complete their development.

Once the system is in working order, a girl's uterus will build up a thick, soft lining each month. An egg will ripen and develop, then be released from one of her ovaries. Each egg contains one set of chromosomes (instead of the two of her other cells). The egg (there is usually just one released at a time) travels down the fallopian tube to the uterus. If it doesn't meet a sperm along the way, the body flushes out the unneeded egg, lining, and extra blood from the uterus through the vagina. This is called a menstrual period and it takes several days to complete each month. Girls may have side effects from this process, including irritability, sadness or other confusing emotions just before her period (called PMS, pre-menstrual syndrome) and sometimes cramping in her abdomen.

During the next few years, both young men and young women will continue to grow and develop physically, as well as spiritually, emotionally, and intellectually, as they prepare for the life of an adult.

The Act of Marriage

Yes, we're finally there. All these changes and developments have a very important point. They prepare our bodies for marriage and childbearing. As we talked about in the last chapter, sex was God's idea and He designed it for marriage. Let's talk about it in a way that hopefully won't tempt you to think about it too much before the time is here. If this section is a temptation to you, skip over it for a better time, or go read it in a room with other people around, so you have some accountability.

The boy and girl have become adults and gotten married to each other. Yeah, we'll talk about how that happens later, too. The husband notices how beautiful his wife is, and trust us, you will think your wife is beautiful, regardless of what the rest of the world thinks of her looks. If he's smart, and our example guy is, he'll tell her how lovely she is. Sweet talk like that leads to hugs and kisses. This progresses to what is called foreplay, where husband and wife explore and caress each other's bodies, especially the parts which are solely for them as mates—the breasts and genitals.

Foreplay causes sexual excitement in both husband and wife. The wife breathes harder, her heart rate increases, her vulva, the area around her vaginal and urethral (where urine comes out) openings swells and her vagina secretes a lubricant. The husband's penis becomes engorged with blood and large and hard. This is why men don't need to worry about the size of their penises. The penis when erect is the correct size, no matter what size it started out. His testicles and prostate gland (located between the bladder and the penis) secrete a small amount of fluids which clean and lubricate the penis. This time of love-making can be steamy and passionate, playful and fun, or gentle and comforting—and is all of those at different times in marriage.

When both husband and wife are sufficiently aroused, they embrace especially closely and the husband inserts his penis into her vagina. This is very pleasurable to both of them. Before long, the husband's body ejaculates and semen is released into his wife's vagina. The hormones that are released, the intimacy and vulnerability of the situation, the emotional and spiritual interaction, all combine to make this a bonding experience like no other. The Bible says that to have sexual relations is to "become one flesh." That's pretty intense language there, but it's true. That's one of the many reasons sex needs to be exclusively between a man and his wife. It's part of their special relationship.

Wait, There's More

That is not the end, though! While the husband and wife bask in each other's love, the sperm are swimming like mad. They will travel up through her cervix (the muscular neck of the uterus that holds a baby in), through her uterus, into her fallopian tubes. If it's the right time and they meet an egg, one sperm will enter the egg, prompting it to change so no other sperm may enter. The nucleus of both sperm and egg join, the DNA combines, and a new person is created—with a completely unique genetic code. Life. New life. God allows us in the intimacy of marriage to be a part of his creation of new life—a new person who's like mom and like dad. A brand new person!

That's another reason sex is for marriage. When a man has relations with a woman he's not married to, he is telling her that satisfying his lust is more important to him than protecting her with his name and commitment to care for the baby that may be conceived. Marriage not only protects the man and woman from sin, but it makes sure there is a family committed to taking care of the baby.

Once the egg is fertilized, that is, it has joined with a sperm and become a living being, it continues traveling down the fallopian tube until it reaches the uterus. There it implants in that nice, soft lining we mentioned earlier. Very soon, the baby starts producing hormones that let mom's body know she is pregnant. In a couple of weeks, when she is expecting her period, she will miss it and if she's paying attention, she could use a pregnancy test which would show that she's expecting a baby! She most likely will not have periods again until some time after the baby is born.

The embryo, which is the scientific name for a baby in these early weeks, forms incredibly quickly. In just a few weeks, the baby is floating in a sack of amniotic fluid attached to the placenta by the umbilical cord. The placenta is an organ that develops during pregnancy to deliver food and oxygen from the mother to the baby. Just four weeks after conception, the baby has a beating heart. Many mothers aren't even sure they're pregnant yet at this point, only two weeks after missing a period.

Starting about 8 weeks after conception, or 10 weeks after mom's last menstrual period, scientists start calling the baby a fetus. During the approximately nine months a baby spends in the mother's uterus, he or she grows and develops. Babies inside the womb can taste some of the things the mother eats as they drink amniotic fluid. They can see light through mom's tummy and hear her voice and other sounds. We divide pregnancy up into three three-month periods of time called trimesters. Sometime in the second trimester, mom will began to feel the baby move, but he's been moving long before she could feel it.

The mother's body goes through a lot of changes. Her blood supply increases by half, her breasts enlarge and develop the capacity to make milk, and the increasing size of the baby begins to show as her "baby bump." Many think a woman is at her most beautiful when she's pregnant.

Congratulations!

Sometime around forty weeks after the mother's last menstrual period (38 weeks after conception), hormones begin to flow that will bring about the baby's birth. The mother's uterus will begin to contract, opening her cervix so that the baby can enter the vagina (at this point, we call it the birth canal, but it's the same thing). This is labor! Typically, the contractions are hardly recognizable at first, but they will grow in strength and frequency until the cervix is open. The last little bit of opening, called transition, can be very challenging for the mother. Having a loving, encouraging husband praying for her and helping her can make it much easier to bear. Once the cervix is open, the uterus, with a lot of help from mom, pushes the baby out. The vagina is incredibly stretchy, so it expands as baby enters, and goes back to normal once the baby is out. The actual birth is usually a time of great joy, pleasure, and happiness.

Once the baby is born, the mother can lift her baby to her breast to cuddle and nurse. This is one of the most exciting times of life—to hold the living, breathing result of our love for our mate is one of the peaks of a lifetime!

Though mom and dad may be distracted with their infant, the placenta soon releases from the uterus and is born, since neither baby nor mama need it anymore. The cord is cut and birth is over. Mama's body will take about six weeks to recover from this huge change. For two to six of those weeks, she'll have a bloody discharge as the lining of her uterus is shed.

Baby, Breastfeeding, and Beyond

Let's get back to the birth, though. Before long the baby is rooting around looking for mom's breasts to nurse. Her breasts are producing colostrum, a golden fluid that comes before her milk comes in. Colostrum contains exactly what the baby needs to begin life outside the womb, including immunities that protect the newborn from infection and even kills germs it directly comes in contact with. Breastmilk, which begins to be produced two to five days after birth, is the perfect food for babies. It provides the right balance of protein and fat to fuel brain growth, immune cells to protect against sickness, and many factors we barely understand that have been found to affect health for the rest of the child's life, including decreasing the risk of asthma, childhood cancers, and diabetes. Breastfeeding provides health benefits for mothers as well: faster recovery from childbirth; drastically reduced rate of breast cancer and other female cancers; reduced risk of diabetes, cardiovascular disease, and arthritis; and reduced expenses as well, since there is no need to buy formula.

Some mothers choose not to breastfeed for a variety of reasons. They may not understand the benefits, they may not have had the support and encouragement they needed, or they may have had difficulties they didn't feel able to overcome. She and her baby will still be fine. If a mother doesn't nurse, her milk will dry up and her breasts return to a non-pregnant, non-nursing state in a few weeks. Her fertility will return and she'll resume regular monthly cycles.

If she does continue breastfeeding her baby, she will usually enjoy a break from ovulating (releasing an egg) and having a monthly cycle, or period. As long as mom is nursing the baby often, not using a pacifier for comfort generally, and nursing more often than every six hours, even at night, her periods and fertility usually don't return until an average of 13 months after childbirth.

Husband and wife usually need to take a break from their physical relationship of sex while the mother is recovering from childbirth, but after six weeks or so, they are ready to resume that part of their relationship. They likely will not conceive again until the mother's period returns or, occasionally, is about to return, then the child-bearing cycle starts all over again, to the great joy of the parents.

Some time when the wife is in her forties or fifties she'll go through yet another hormonal change. Her period will become irregular, she might have hot flashes or other symptoms and eventually her period will stop and she'll no longer be fertile. The sexual relationship of marriage continues, though, and husbands do not go through a similar change.

What's the Point?

Why did we spend all this time explaining the biology of reproduction? We know it seems pretty complicated, and you wouldn't believe the amount of detail *we left out!* We want you to understand, though, that it's not just about the few minutes of actual sexual intercourse. Sex is part of a whole cycle of life that begins at conception and ends at death. In a way, it even continues past that, as the children conceived through this special act outlive us.

We want to satisfy your curiosity about sexuality. We also want you to appreciate that it's all connected. Having sex is a part of marriage and childbearing and love and trust and bonding. It's not something you can just do carelessly. It's way more important—and way better than that. Save it for when it matters. Save it for what it was made for. You'll be glad—because it is very good.

Summary

- Gender is decided at conception and boys and girls are different. Of course.

- Puberty brings a host of changes and they aren't all physical.

- Sex is just one part of a huge cycle of marriage, childbearing, and life.

- Sex is meant for bonding, enjoyment, and the creation of new life.

- Marriage protects everyone—husband, wife, and child.

- Sexuality is fun, passionate, and even beautiful in the context God designed it for—marriage.

3

THE ENEMY PERVERTS GOD'S DESIGN

Sin, Hook-ups, Gender-bending, Porn

We once had a mixed-breed dog which was part Labrador. We love our Labs; they're loyal, easy-going, friendly dogs. The other half of this particular mutt was the wild card—she was half beagle. Martha was a sweet-natured dog (we gave credit to her Labrador father), but beagles are tracking dogs which are bred for sensitive noses and—can we say "dogged"?—persistence when hunting.

Martha was a reasonably obedient dog, but if she *ever* caught wind of a prey animal, whether it was an elderly possum or a massive buck, her drive to chase and capture took over her entire body. Wow, how that dog could run! We used to say there was a direct connection between her nose and her toes, totally bypassing her brain. Trying to catch her or call her home was fruitless; the instinct was simply too strong to deny.

We are not dogs, and God specifically calls us to live in a thoughtful, self-controlled way. Still, our sexual drive is remarkably strong, and it can become overwhelming if we give it free rein. Sexual desires not only play a part in the creation of life and the continuation of humanity on our planet, but these feelings can also engage our minds, hearts, and bodies more strongly than almost any other stimulus.

That means that, when harnessed and working in the paths God directs, sexuality is a deep fountain of joy and excitement, and can even provide encouragement and motivation we can carry into our daily life.

It also means we are sorely tempted to chase those feelings and sensations down any road which offers to provide more, just like our beagle-lab mix would run until she was lost or even in danger.

The challenge is that we are given a narrow pathway for those feelings and sensations —marriage, and marriage only. The Bible contains hundreds of prohibitions against sexual sin. It warns of spiritual, physical, emotional, and social consequences for sexual immorality. Under the Law of Moses which governed ancient Israel, the law which God gave them, many of these sins carried a death penalty. God created this awesome, powerful thing in our human frame, and He intends for us to keep it in line—and He really means it.

God expects us to stay within the boundaries of sexual morality the same as we stay inside His borders for other behaviors. When He says, *"Do not steal,"* He doesn't hedge to say, "Don't steal, but I'll look the other way if you're poor and the rightful owner can afford to lose it" (in fact, the Bible specifically says the opposite). He doesn't excuse theft if the victim is a big corporation, or a corrupt government, or an exploitive employer; He says very simply and directly, *"Do not steal."* [1]

The Bible observes that *"God made man upright, But they have sought out many schemes."* [2] We look for loopholes and gaps in the fence. Just as the thief may rationalize his stealing by thinking he's poor and his victim is rich, or that he's only taking back what ought to be his anyway, we also create a book full of hopeful excuses for our sexual sin. We tell ourselves that no one will know, or that no one is really hurt, or that the other person agreed, so it's consensual... and hope God doesn't hold it against us.

If we can be honest with God and ourselves, we can start to make progress identifying where the traps are placed and setting out a game plan for avoiding them ... or breaking free, if we're already caught.

---

1 The Eighth Commandment is found in Exodus 20:15. Proverbs 6:30-31 reads, "People *do not despise a thief If he steals to satisfy himself when he is starving. Yet* when *he is found, he must restore sevenfold; He may have to give up all the substance of his house."*

2 Ecclesiastes 7:29

History and the Culture Aren't Helping Us

While God has ordained the proper channel for your sexual energy, through your marriage and focused on your wife, you've already discovered that curiosity and temptation in sexual matters begin long before you reach a marriageable age. Your first challenge is living a godly life as a single man.

That's a real challenge, no matter how long it lasts, but unfortunately, the usual period of singleness is lengthening every year. That means the battle is lasting longer and longer.

For one thing, boys are starting puberty earlier than before. One obvious sign of the physical changes underway is when a young man's voice breaks— that awkward period when his voice skips from a youthful tenor to a squeak, and when he's still likely to be mistaken for his mother when he answers the phone at home.

In the centuries after the Protestant Reformation, the great masterpieces of church music did not include women's parts. They used boys' choirs to sing the high notes, the soprano and alto voices which are usually sung by women today. In the early 1700's J.S. Bach was the music director at St. Thomas Church in Leipzig, Germany. He knew that a boy's voice would change between 17 and 18 years old, and maybe even as late as 19 or 20.

The Boys Choir at the St. Thomas Church still exists today, but the manager recently told *The Washington Post* they are finding boys "crack" as young as 13 today. The school had to add primary grades in order to identify, recruit, and train singers between 9 and 12 years old; otherwise they'll lose the boys' soprano voices altogether. The Copenhagen Municipal Choir School in Denmark is facing a similar problem, saying the change is coming six months earlier than just a generation ago. It's affecting their ability to perform, since the younger singers haven't had the life experience to relate to the emotional power of the music.[3]

At the same time, the age when men get married has been climbing. According to the U.S. Census Bureau, in 1970 the median age of first marriage for

---

3 Michael Birnbaum, "Leipzig's St. Thomas Boys Choir Copes with Voices Deepening at a Younger Age." *Washington Post* 7 April 2012: n. pag. *The Washington Post*, 07 Apr 2012.

men was 24; by 2010, it was over 28 and trending toward 29.[4] There are many factors which play into this, of course, including several years of a difficult economy and a tendency to expect longer periods of education before starting a career. The number of couples choosing to live together rather than commit to marriage is climbing as well, to the point where more than half of adults under the age of fifty have cohabited at some point.[5]

The end of the matter is this: Young men are becoming sexually aware at younger ages, and at the same time, beginning married life older and older. When puberty starts at 16 and marriage occurs at 22, there's a period of six years when a young man is dealing with sexual feelings and has no God-given outlet for them. But with puberty starting as early as 10, according to some researchers, and marriage moving closer to 30, a young man is facing a long battle indeed. By the time he walks the aisle with his bride, a virtuous young man has spent most of his life fighting this battle.

Giving Up and Giving In

From all indications, most guys are losing the fight—if they ever even engaged it. While they might choose earlier marriage rather than later, if possible, they can't do much about biology that makes the battle longer. Instead of resisting that temptation, too many are engaging in sexual activity outside of marriage. Statistics show increasing rates of cohabitation and childbirth out of wedlock, and an explosion of involvement with pornography and sex-related business. It is no longer the norm for adults to be married, or for children to have parents who are married to each other. Over 90% of young men have been exposed to pornography by the age of 18, and nearly 75% are sexually active by the age of 19.[6]

The consequences are already apparent in society. One of our sons wrote back from college recently and said, "I was realizing that, talking the other day with a few guys, I was the only person at the table who had two *biological, married*

---

4 Diana B. Elliott, Kristy Krivickas, Matthew W. Brault, and Rose M. Kreider, "Historical Marriage Trends from 1890-2010: A Focus on Race Differences." Presentation to the Population Association of America, San Francisco, May 3-5, 2012. Figure 1, p. 13.

5 Kennedy, Sheela, and Larry Bumpass. "Cohabitation and children's living arrangements: New estimates from the United States." *Demographic Research*. 19. (2008): 1663-1692.

6 Sabina *et al.*

parents." He shared how his economics professor asked class members what it would take to maximize their happiness. One student answered, "I'd like to have a family, and be the dad I didn't have, and enough money to pay the bills."

That's a noble goal, but heartbreaking to hear it expressed as his ultimate desire, not just assumed as something that would definitely happen.

God's design for our lives has not changed, and His call for personal purity has not ended. Yes, it's difficult, and getting worse all around us. Yet Paul the apostle gave this encouragement to the beleaguered believers at Corinth:

> *No temptation has overtaken you except such as is common to man; but God is faithful, who will not allow you to be tempted beyond what you are able, but with the temptation will also make the way of escape, that you may be able to bear it.*[7]

So don't despair—there are ways to carry on this fight for your own sexual purity and win! It is not a lost cause ... even if you've fallen before. There is hope and there is help.

Thoughts and Feelings Count

What is our fundamental problem? In sexual areas and in everything else, we have a natural tendency to run from God and seek our own pleasure rather than His. Several denominations define sin as "any want of conformity unto, or transgression of, the law of God."[8] In other words, sin is whenever we fail to do what God commands, whether we intentionally disobey Him or if we neglect to pay attention and do what He tells us.

So we are born with a desire to sin. In sexual areas, this comes up as lust. This is a deep desire for something which we should not have—the same word, in the Greek New Testament, is sometimes translated "covet." It is not covetous to admire a beautiful sports car on the road and think, "Wow, I'd like to be able to afford one of those one day." It would be coveting indeed if you filled your waking thoughts with images of that car, and yearned and pined over it to the harm of your soul.

---

7 1 Corinthians 10:13

8 Westminster Shorter Catechism, Q.14 ("What is sin?")

Likewise, it is not lust for a married man to admire the beauty of his wife and wish to be intimate with her. The Bible says that her body belongs to him (and his body to her, too), and they are *commanded* to enjoy one another sexually.[9] Thinking about it beforehand is no sin for either one!

It is not even, necessarily, a sinful lust for an unmarried young man to notice the beauty of an unmarried young woman. In Genesis 29, Jacob was frankly bowled over by the sight of Rachel, who was *"beautiful of form and appearance."* [10] There's no indication of *lust* here, but there certainly was a sudden willingness to take a seven-year commitment in order to win this beauty for his bride![11]

To indulge a sexual desire for someone other than your wife, though, to look at their beauty and think over all the sensual possibilities that might include— that, indeed, is lust.

The Bible says a lot about immoral sexual acts, but it warns us to *"Flee also youthful lusts,"* as Paul wrote to Timothy.[12] He told the Roman church to *"put on the Lord Jesus Christ, and make no provision for the flesh, to* fulfill *its lusts."* [13] The grace of God teaches us that, *"denying ungodliness and worldly lusts, we should live soberly, righteously, and godly in the present age."*[14] Of course we know to avoid immoral *acts*, but God expects us to be more holy than that. His bar is set higher, or you might say, the line in the sand is a lot sooner than we tend to think.

Lust itself takes different forms. Sometimes it is a secret, internal thing which lives and coils around our heart and mind, but hides itself from others' view. Sometimes it is plain to all and displayed to the world.

We were recently at a conference at the beach. One of our friends stood by the edge of the surf to take a photo with her phone. Suddenly a bigger than usual wave struck her and caused her to stumble. Her bag, phone, and all

---

9 1 Corinthians 7:2-5

10 Genesis 29:17-18

11 It's reasonable to ask why Jacob didn't offer to serve seven years *following* the wedding, rather than before. It may simply be evidence of how a young man can be so distracted by a girl he can't think straight. Keep this in mind.

12 2 Timothy 2:22

13 Romans 13:14

14 Titus 2:12

splashed into the seawater. Lust is not merely a little forbidden place that we can carefully sidestep, but rather it's a rolling tide which can wash over us if we wander—or run—too close. And it ends badly. The apostle John, late in his life, wrote to the people,

> Do not love the world or the things of the world. If anyone loves the world, the love of the Father is not in him. For all that is in the world— the lust of the flesh, the lust of the eyes, and the pride of life—is not of the Father but is of the world. And the world is passing away, and the lust of it; but he who does the will of God abides forever.[15]

We are all tempted at different times, and sometimes tempted *hard.* It's important (and comforting) to remember that *temptation* is not sin. The English Puritan, Thomas Brooks, noted that "God had but one Son without corruption, but He had none without temptation." The point is what we do with temptation—do we embrace it, act on it, dream about it? Or do we recognize it for what it is—our own sinfulness, or an attack by the Tempter, which is nothing but a trap for our souls—and then with God's help, turn away from its attraction?

The Rising Tide of Pornography

One of the most prevalent—and dangerous—traps today is one of the oldest: pornography.

Pictures of sexual activity have been found on ancient walls, antique vases, and other very old objects and locations. Apparently, man has been lifting the veil on this most private act as long as he's been drawing. It's nothing new.

In your parents' or grandparents' generation, if a young man wanted to peer at pornography, there were ways to accomplish it. It might involve sneaking a look behind the magazine rack, or shoplifting a copy of a "men's magazine," or discovering where an uncle or older cousin may have hidden his stash. It could be done, but it took some nerve and some risk, and much of it (the motion picture side) was nearly impossible for a teenager to access.

Now the industry has moved online, and it is literally no further away than a couple of links or a mistyped URL. In the last generation, a boy had to work hard to find pornography. Now, that boy's grown up, and he and his son have

---

15 1 John 2:15-17

to work even harder to keep pornography *away*. It's pushed its way into the margins and sidebars of legitimate websites, so the bait is displayed right next to the news, sports, or hobby information.

The most important thing to remember, Biblically, is that Jesus addressed this temptation directly. In the Sermon on the Mount, He warned that *"whoever looks at a woman to lust for her"* —a good definition of what pornography is offering—*"whoever looks at a woman to lust for her has already committed adultery with her in his heart."*[16]

There are many, many men who would never *dream* of hiring a prostitute or having an extramarital affair, men who protest that they love their wives—who are still committing adultery. We recently read that 56% of divorce cases involve one spouse's "obsessive interest in pornographic websites"[17] and half of Christian men in a 2006 survey were found to have pornography addiction.[18]

And there are many unmarried young men, even in their teens, who intend to keep themselves pure for marriage and would never try to sleep with their girlfriend—yet on their phones and laptops, are filling their eyes and minds with lust. Jesus calls that adultery.

Let's be honest with ourselves, too—if God looks on the heart and judges our thoughts as well as our actions (and He does), then the secret images and imaginations we cherish are liable for His righteous anger, as well. Too often we try to minimize our sin by thinking, "Nobody else is involved," or "I'm not actually *doing* that, just fantasizing about it in my head."

Yet, Jesus clearly says that while we all understand that actually having a sexual affair outside of marriage is a sin, it is also a sin to stir up the lust which comes earlier along the pathway. In the same sermon Jesus said that just as it is a sin to murder someone, it is a sin to seethe with unrighteous anger which might lead to murder in the end—so you see the pattern: God is concerned with the invisible pursuits of our heart as well as the outward actions we take.[19]

---

16 Matthew 5:27-28

17 American Academy of Matrimonial Lawyers, cited in *Pornography Statistics* (Owosso, MI: Covenant Eyes, 2014), p. 12

18 Poll by ChristiaNet, cited in *Pornography Statistics,* p. 20.

19 Matthew 5:21-22

For the word of God is living and powerful, and sharper than any
two-edged sword, piercing even to the division of soul and spirit, and
of joints and marrow, and is a discerner of the thoughts and intents
of the heart. And there is no creature hidden from His sight, but all
things are naked and open to the eyes of Him to whom we must give
account.[20]

I, the LORD, search the heart, I test the mind, Even to give every man
according to his ways, According to the fruit of his doings.[21]

Never a Victimless Crime

Pornography, and many other sexual sins, are sometimes excused as "victimless crimes." This is patently false, and here's the toll:

1. Sexual sin victimizes the sinner first

We already spoke about the problem of lust, which is the evil desire which underlies sexual misbehavior, both great and small. Before there is sexual assault, before there is prostitution, before there is any "acting out" at all, there is a cave-in to the promptings of lust. We've already shown what Jesus and the Bible say about this sin.

There's more, though. The apostle Paul warned the church in Corinth that sexual sin is different than other transgressions:

Flee sexual immorality. Every sin that a man does is outside the body,
but he who commits sexual immorality sins against his own body.[22]

It's enough that Scripture tells us this fact, but science is confirming it. Medical professionals are reporting an explosion of impotence, sexual dysfunction, among young adult men. It's being traced to pornography use, which causes the viewer's brain to become desensitized to the stimulating hormones in normal sexual activity. At a time of life when their testosterone (and sexual desire) is at a peak, their bodies are malfunctioning because of the abuse they've inflicted on themselves.

---

20 Hebrews 4:12-13

21 Jeremiah 17:10

22 1 Corinthians 6:18

So even for private sins of lust, there is at least one victim.

2. Those who provide the opportunity for lust are also victims.

Pornography de-personalizes the sexual act and makes the actors and actresses into mere symbols and props. Many of the people who appear in these images are living in practical slavery, often addicted to drugs and alcohol to dampen the revulsion they feel toward themselves and their employment. By consuming these images, even those which are "free," the viewer provides the market which keeps the industry going—for selling the advertising if not the product itself.

3. Women in general, and the culture as well, are degraded by the use of pornography.

The expansion in the use of pornography cheapens the honor and protection shown toward women and girls. The very nature of the beast is to make women into objects and trophies, and even if you don't personally use pornography, its effects bleed over into the culture. The gray area where "soft core" pornography overlaps into "polite" culture is shaped by the undercurrents of obscenity below, and society's definition of what makes a woman beautiful or desirable is influenced by the industry. Clothing styles which were considered risqué a few generations ago are marketed for little girls now, and the sexualization of pre-teen girlhood is directly related to the increase in demand for child pornography. When a culture doesn't even protect children, it's very bad indeed.

4. Pornography creates expectations which will be impossible for your wife to meet.

One of the makers of facial care products produced a remarkable video that followed a rather plain-featured model as she was transformed by professional makeup and hair styling, a studio photo session, and extensive retouching of the digital image. The glamorous result was intended for billboard display, and once every stray hair, tiny freckle, or miniature wrinkle was erased, the glamorous image didn't have much resemblance to the real woman. Pornography is marketing of a special sort—the sale of lust—and the producer who has no scruples about placing men and women in the most degrading and de-humanizing situations for the camera, certainly has no concern over retouching anything and everything. Some of the women presented online don't even exist in reality, and in some cases the image has been so doctored up, an actual person with those characteristics couldn't even stand properly.

In contrast, a real-life, healthy woman, just like her husband, won't be "perfect." She'll have her own individuality of appearance—freckles, birthmarks, a scar from a childhood accident, a stretch mark from pregnancy, and a bad hair day now and then. These aren't blemishes, but simply the traces of life being lived out. There is no way a real woman can compare with the airbrushed image of a digitally-enhanced modeling session—and she shouldn't be expected to try.

The medium also presents a twisted fantasy of sexual behavior. A regular viewer of pornography is led to think that women are eager for physical abuse, sexual aggression, and generally being treated like a prostitute or a harem slave. (This soul-killing scenario accounts for the rampant drug use among pornographic actresses, by the way.)

So a young man who feeds on this sort of image is training himself to desire a woman who doesn't exist in real life. He'll be disappointed to find that his bride isn't a she-tiger with an unlimited appetite for sex, but an actual woman with feelings that can be hurt, with expectations of her own, and a dignity which can be easily destroyed by a callous lover. Sooner or later, his wife will be the victim of his pornographic training.

Is that your dream for the young woman you hope to marry?

Sexting: Think Before You Answer the Phone

Technology has changed other ways we're tempted too. Things which used to take professionals a week to do with rooms full of equipment and large operating budgets, we now can accomplish in minutes, for free. And our ever-present little phones, which make us older folk feel like Captain Kirk from *Star Trek*, are turning high school students into amateur pornographers.

How? By using their phones to take sexually explicit or suggestive photos of themselves or each other, then passing them around for fun or spite. You don't even have to have a particularly smart phone to be "sexting"—just a camera and enough bandwidth to attach a picture to a text message.

The evil inherent to this whole idea ought to be obvious. It's a sin to be inflaming yourself with lust over the image of another person's body. It's also a sin to be leading others into that lust.

But there's another catch—if the person in the image is under 18, *even if it's yourself*, then you could be guilty of producing or receiving child pornography. High school students and younger have been prosecuted for having suggestive pictures of a classmate on their phones, and it's a felony offense which makes headlines.[23] The law hasn't kept up with the changing technology (or the erosion of popular morals), and it doesn't distinguish between the sweaty porn photographer in a mildewed studio, and teenagers exchanging "edgy" prank photos on their phones. Pictures of nude minors are child pornography, and that's that.

A child porn charge on the record is not a good way to set out in adult life, to say the least.

Just as the Internet has made pornography an explosively growing business even in Christian circles, the practice of sexting is working its way into mainstream student life. The trap is that once an image or text is released in a digital world, it is nearly impossible to call it back. More and more young people are finding that a "flirtatious" message or photo that was intended to be private has acquired a life of its own, appearing on social media, phone-to-phone messaging, and other channels. Young women in particular are finding the reputation damage is lasting and deeply disturbing. Some have even taken their own lives in response to the harassment that follows.

This is something you want no part of, whether creating, sending, or receiving it. That means you need to be careful who you give your phone number to. You can choose not to open an attachment on an email, but by the time you view a text, it is too late. The image is in your mind and can tempt you from now on.

That means that you don't take pictures like that and you don't let anyone else take a picture of you like that. One mother told us she put a photo-sharing app on their family's phones, only to find out her teen son had taken inappropriate photos and shared them with friends. That's trafficking in child pornography and it's a serious felony. Their family was shaken to the core.

---

23 Martha Irvine, "Porn charges for 'sexting' stir debate." The Associated Press, 2009. From NBC News, *http://www.nbcnews.com/id/29017808/*, accessed 8/27/14.

Words Are Powerful, Too

While we're thinking about text, don't underestimate the danger of the written word. Most guys are so bombarded by the fleshy click-bait on the screen, they don't bother with trashy novels. In fact, women are much more likely to be caught by the text-based pornography than the visual sort; one survey found a majority of girls were "disgusted" by the visual porn they'd seen, and very few found it exciting at all.[24]

But that temptation is still there, and while its impact may be blunted a bit—the images you form while reading are limited by your own experience or exposure, to some extent—it can still be a powerful incitement to lust. That, after all, is the root of the problem, isn't it—to indulge a desire for something which would be sinful to do or have?

This should guide you in your choice of reading material, whether it's news stories or full-length novels. It should be obvious that salacious books are not always the ones with half-nude people on the covers, or hidden behind the cash register wrapped in plastic. In fact, it's often military or spy fiction that includes that kind of thing because they know it appeals to men. You have to use some discernment about the content and the basic premise of the story.

And when you accidentally stumble across heavy breathing passages in an otherwise acceptable book, there's a radical solution: skip them, or quit the book. Honestly, avid readers sometimes have a hard time breaking off in the middle of book, as if they get virtue points for reading all the words both good and bad. It's not finishing your vegetables at the dinner table, guys; you're feeding your mind and through it, your soul, and when you find the food has gone rancid, *it's time to stop.*

Masturbation

One area that is dividing teachers in the Christian church is the practice of masturbation. Once it was uniformly condemned, sometimes with exaggerated warnings of consequences. Now there are respected Christian leaders who condone the practice, saying it's no more problematic than scratching an

---

24 Chiara, Sabina, Janis Wolak, and David Finkelhor. "The Nature and Dynamics of Internet Pornography Exposure for Youth." CyberPsychology & Behavior. 11.6 (2008): n. page. Web. 2 Sep. 2012 <http://www.unh.edu/ccrc/pdf/CV169.pdf>.

itch. Sometimes, we think, they allow it with thanks that it's not something worse.

It is true that the Bible does not give a clear "Thou shalt not" on the subject. There are other sins which get that specific treatment—things like adultery, which involves the deepest sort of deception and betrayal in addition to the sexual impurity of the act. Even without an eleventh commandment or Jesus discussing the matter with the disciples, though, there are principles in Scripture which lead us to say masturbation is not okay.

First is the fundamental nature of sex, which is centered on marriage. God created the sexual act in the process of creating Adam and Eve, and He immediately brought them together in the first marriage with instructions to use this gift. The sexual union is an expression of the spiritual union of husband and wife, and it carries the prospect of conceiving new life. It is something to be shared, but exclusively between the man and woman who have made a lifelong commitment to one another. It is meant to be private, but there is no shame.

Masturbation is none of these. It is solitary, furtive, and unfruitful. It involves no one but the self and whatever fantasy images are pursued at the time. And it frequently produces a sense of guilt or shame in the process.

Frankly, there are no passages of Scripture which suggest that sexual sensations are okay to pursue in any other channel than marriage or with any person other than your spouse in mind. There is nothing to suggest that sexual sensation is meant for solitary amusement, without even the slightest chance of bringing a child into the world.

Even more, the New Testament points firmly in a different direction. The apostle Paul was apparently married at one point in his life—he had been a member of the Sanhedrin, the Jewish ruling council, which held marriage as a qualification for its members—but during his missionary years was single again.[25] *"Do we have no right to take along a believing wife, as* do *also the other apostles?"* he asked at one point.[26] He acknowledged that in his transient ministry life, he faced dangers when he traveled and persecution where he stopped. In his case, there were advantages to singleness:

---

25 The Bible does not elaborate whether he was divorced or widowed, so there's no point in speculating.

26 1 Corinthians 9:5

"I suppose therefore," he wrote to Corinth, *"that this is good because of the present distress—that* it is *good for a man to remain as he is..."*[27] whether married or not. *"I say to the unmarried and to the widows: it is good for them if they remain even as I am ... He who is unmarried cares for the things of the Lord—how he may please the Lord. But he who is married cares about the things of this world—how he may please his wife."*[28]

So Paul, who had been single then married then single again, saw distinct advantages for ministry and service to God in his single state. What did he say to believers struggling in the oversexed culture of Corinth? They lived in a city known for its prostitution and open homosexual display. How should they manage their temptations and desires in a culture with many of the same struggles as our own?

It would have been so easy for him to say, "Brethren, it's just a physical urge like hunger or thirst. It's a distraction. Go off someplace private, take care of it yourself, and then get back to work and ministry."

But Paul says the exact opposite. In the midst of his encouragement about serving God while single, Paul says very plainly,

"Nevertheless, because of sexual immorality, let each man have his own wife ... Let the husband render to his wife the affection due her ... [and] Do not deprive one another except with consent for a time, that you may give yourselves to fasting and prayer; and come together again so that Satan does not tempt you because of your lack of self-control."[29]

Remember that ancient Corinth was a place where sexual activity and promiscuity were taken for granted by the public at large. It was much like our country today. Paul gives the believer two choices—self-controlled celibacy, or marriage. Pursuing sexual excitement and release as a private act is not an option.

Furthermore, when the church was spreading across the Roman Empire, this unmarried apostle did *not* hold up singleness as the ideal for leadership. When

---

27 1 Corinthians 7:26

28 1 Corinthians 7:8, 32, 33

29 1 Corinthians 7:2, 3, 5

he related the qualifications for ordained church officers, he didn't point to celibacy but marriage: it was a requirement for bishops,[30] elders,[31] and deacons alike.[32]

If self-gratifying sexual recreation were an acceptable answer to those desires, why wouldn't the apostle recommend it as a way to help hot-blooded young men keep their minds on celibate ministry? It would certainly be much less trouble and distraction than pursuing and wedding a wife and caring for her and the children ... yet the married life is *precisely* what the apostle recommends.

Is It Self-Abuse?

In polite circles, masturbation used to be called "self-abuse," and it's understandable why a modern reader would balk at that characterization. How could it be abusive if it doesn't injure anybody, or even involve anybody but the "abuser" himself?

It helps to understand the older definition of the term "abuse." It doesn't mean torture or mutilation; it means "to use wrongly" or "to misuse." If you pry open a paint can with a screwdriver, it's true you might not damage the tool, but it's not meant for that purpose. In that situation, you are misusing, or abusing, the screwdriver.

Likewise, over-stimulating yourself in this way is misusing the gift of sexuality as God gave it. There is no bonding or union because there is no wife involved. There is no fulfillment of the command to fill the earth with descendants. It is a supremely selfish act, completely self-centered.

And like all sexual sin, this harms the sinner first. The reality is that self-stimulation attempts to drive the physical cycle of sexual response far beyond the normal relations of husband and wife. There is a natural ebb and flow in the marriage relationship, just like tides and seasons. Although marriage provides the God-given outlet for sexual desire, it's not possible to satisfy those desires whenever you feel like it. There are constraints of health, fatigue, busyness, or even just time and privacy.

---

30 1 Timothy 3:2

31 Titus 1:5-6

32 1 Timothy 3:12

If your only concern is your own desire, these relationship issues are minimal or non-existent. Pornography allows the user to fill his mind with rapidly changing or endlessly repeating images, far beyond anything he'd ever witness first hand. Masturbation does the same thing in the body, providing an unnatural level of physical stimulation the body isn't equipped to handle. Either way, the overload damages the brain's ability to even enjoy the sensations it seeks, and it leads to deeper and more degrading sins. (Take that as given, and we'll discuss why that happens, medically, later.)

Ask yourself—if that's not abuse, misusing something to the point of damaging it, what is? It certainly bears out what Paul warned the Corinthians—*"Every sin that a man does is outside the body, but he who commits sexual immorality sins against his own body."* [33]

IRL

We all know the text-message acronym, IRL—"In Real Life"—which distinguishes our online conversation and friendship from one-on-one, flesh-and-blood, face-to-face interaction. We may have two thousand friends on Facebook, but only our friends IRL will show up for the wedding.

We've spent most of this chapter warning about the kinds of traps that catch us when we're alone. You can have a problem with sexual sin while marooned on a desert island, with no girl within a thousand miles.

Now what about "real life"? Where are the boundaries in our actual person-to-person moments?

The Bible is abundantly clear that sexual intercourse is reserved for marriage. The husband or wife who engages in sex with someone else after they're married is committing adultery, violating the seventh commandment (Exodus 20:14). The unmarried person who has sex is committing fornication[34]. Sexual relations beyond the normal, involving same-sex attraction, close relatives, or even non-persons, are strictly off limits.

But what about a guy and girl who don't plan to go "all the way," as they used to say? What does the Bible say about that?

---

33 1 Corinthians 6:18

34 I Corinthians 6:15-20

We know what the culture says about that—the world wants to believe it doesn't count if you're not actually having intercourse. When President Clinton was caught having an affair with a young White House intern, he tried to brazen it out by declaring, "I did not have sex with that woman." It may be true that he didn't take her to bed in the classic sense, but it became very public that they were engaging in other forms of sexual expression which still violated God's law—because the standard is to avoid lust, not only specific acts or relationships.

That should be your rule of thumb when you consider your interaction with girls. Are you finding your desire rising in a situation or activity? Then it's time to back down. Are you thinking more about her figure or parts of her body than about her thoughts and words? Is she becoming more of an object of desire and less of a whole person in your mind? Are you starting to rationalize or justify the next step in your physical relationship? Then you need to be on guard.

Gender Questions

We live in a time of gender fluidity, where people seem to assume that a person can be born a man in a woman's body or a woman in a man's body or a man attracted to other men or a woman attracted to other women or both. We hear folks saying that everyone deserves a chance to be happy, everyone deserves love, that all these different kinds of sexuality really don't hurt anyone, so we ought to stay out of it. What does the Word of God say, though?

Gender as male and female is not some accident of chance, but a creation of God:

> So God created man in his own image, in the image of God he created him; male and female he created them.[35]

Biology bears that out. Every cell in our bodies (with the exception of half of the sperm), contains the DNA that defines our gender. So, if you are male, even your hair and nails are male. The Scripture shows us that God intends for us to stick to that gender, too.

The Old Testament warns against both cross-dressing[36] and homosexuality. In fact, it goes beyond warning to say,

35 Genesis 1:27

36 Deuteronomy 22:5

You shall not lie with a male as with a woman; it is an abomination.[37]

Many people remind us that we're not bound to the ceremonial law of the Old Testament, but this is moral law. We know that for sure, because it is taught again in the New Testament. Speaking of man's willful rejection of God, the apostle Paul wrote:

> *For this reason God gave them up to dishonorable passions. For their women exchanged natural relations for those that are contrary to nature; and the men likewise gave up natural relations with women and were consumed with passion for one another, men committing shameless acts with men and receiving in themselves the due penalty for their error.*[38]

What about people who say they've always had a feeling they should have been a different sex or always had sexual desire for the same sex? Well, some people are born with a temptation to anger or to greed, no doubt, but it is not an excuse for sin.

The good news is that if those sexual acts are sin that means that you do not have to be that way. That you can, with the help of God, be freed from it. The Good News is still the good news!

---

37 Leviticus 18:22

38 Romans 1:26-27 ESV

Summary

- Sexuality is powerful by design, and we can be tempted to pursue it down the wrong paths.

- Sexual desires are only meant to be satisfied in marriage.

- The root of the problem is lust, and anything which stirs it up needs to be avoided.

- In sexual behavior, there is no such thing as a "victimless crime."

- Early puberty and late marriage are lengthening the fight

4

How Can a Young Man Keep His Way Pure?

Practical Ways to Fight Temptation

When you read about all the ways Satan is tempting you to go astray, it can be pretty discouraging. You start thinking, "Everybody is doing it. How can I stay out of sin when hardly anyone does?" We've got to remember this:

> Enter by the narrow gate; for wide is the gate and broad is the way that leads to destruction, and there are many who go in by it. Because narrow is the gate and difficult is the way which leads to life, and there are few who find it.[1]

So, yeah, few people do the right thing. That doesn't mean you can't. It just means it's going to be a challenge.

God has promised us, though, that it is not impossible.

> No temptation has overtaken you except such as is common to man; but God is faithful, who will not allow you to be tempted beyond what you are able, but with the temptation will also make the way of escape, that you may be able to bear it.[2]

---

1 Matthew 7:13-14
2 1 Corinthians 10:13

That means it is not too strong for you. You *can* help it. You do not have to do it.

You just need some practical help. Here goes.

A Fist to Knock Away Temptation

We tell our guys that there are five good ways to fight sexual temptation, or really, any temptation.

Get out of the situation

That's pretty obvious, but we forget about it. If you're in the shower, dry off and get out. If you are in your room alone, get up and go where there are other people.

It is not a failure to admit that the ground is slippery or deep in sucking mud; head for a different path. Remember the example of Joseph, whose master's wife tried to seduce him; when she tried to pull him into her arms, he wriggled out of his robe and fled.[3] The commentator Matthew Henry remarked drily, "It is better to lose a good coat than a good conscience."[4]

When Hal was working as an engineer in the power industry, he was trained to avoid error-likely situations. He was told that if there were factors that made mistakes more likely, for example, if you were sick or short on sleep, or working on a new system, or in a storm, you needed to be particularly careful. In the power industry, a mistake can shut off the power to a whole town—or kill a coworker.

When it comes to our sexuality, mistakes can change your life and your children's lives, so we need to watch out for error-likely situations, too. We remember being young and in love and walking all over campus late at night, just so we could talk a little more. Being sleepy and tired, though, is an error-likely situation. It makes it more likely you will say too much or do things you wouldn't otherwise do because your judgment is off. It's best not to be alone when you are tired, sleepy, and tempted.

---

3 Genesis 39:11-12
4 Matthew Henry, "Commentary on Genesis 39." Blue Letter Bible.

One of the great lies of the enemy is that "no one will ever know." Now, that's a lie on the face of it, because

> *O LORD, you have searched me and known me!*
> *You know when I sit down and when I rise up;*
>   *you discern my thoughts from afar.*[5]

and

> *Therefore we also, since we are surrounded by so great a cloud of witnesses, let us lay aside every weight, and the sin which so easily ensnares us, and let us run with endurance the race that is set before us...*[6]

When we are alone, though, we make this lie easier to believe. So, if you're alone with a young woman and you are tempted, get the two of you in public. Say something like "Hey, let's go grab some dinner," or "Why don't we walk up to the student center?" If you are alone and you are being tempted to porn, fantasy or masturbation, get out of there and get with other people. Sometimes we have to go find some accountability. That's okay. Wisdom says that *"A prudent man foresees evil and hides himself."*[7]

Pray to God

Imagine this. A young officer is out on the edge of the battle leading a group of men trying to get far enough to the side to take the enemy in flank. They round the hill only to see evidence men have been here before. "Sir, shall I ride for reinforcements," his aide says.

"No, son, I don't want to holler for help at the first sign of trouble." As they clear the hill, shots begin to ring out. There are snipers in the trees!

"Sir, they know we're here! Shall I ride for help?"

"No, Private, we can handle a few snipers. I don't want them to think I can't handle a little set back," but as his troops move into the clear, an overwhelming force meets them. The shock pushes them back.

"Captain! Shall I ride for the reserves?" his aide gasps out.

---

5 Psalm 139:1-2 ESV
6 Hebrews 12:1
7 Proverbs 22:3 and again in 27:12

"It's too late to ask for help. Besides, I think I can do this," the captain answers right before he was taken down.

We'd think this was a pretty foolish young man, wouldn't we?

We do the same thing, though, when we neglect to ask the Lord for help.

When we fall into temptation, we should pray to God for help to resist. Jesus taught us to pray, *Do not lead us into temptation, But deliver us from the evil one.*[8] He *gave Himself for our sins, that He might deliver us from this present evil age ...*[9] The psalmist wrote, *The eyes of the LORD are on the righteous, and His ears are open to their cry ...* The righteous *cry out, and the LORD hears, and delivers them out of all their troubles,*[10] and *The LORD shall preserve you from all evil ...*[11]

So, don't be the soldier who dies on the battlefield too proud to call out to his King for reinforcements. Instead, pray and ask for help.

Read Your Bible

We can take our minds off the temptation by soaking it with God's Word. We even see God's Word portrayed as an offensive weapon against the enemy. *For the word of God is living and powerful, and sharper than any two-edged sword ... and is a discerner of the thoughts and intents of the heart.*[12] If you don't have a Bible handy, quote Scripture to yourself—anything you may have memorized. *How can a young man cleanse his way? By taking heed according to Your word. ... Your word I have hidden in my heart, That I might not sin against You.*[13]

Hal has found it very helpful in times of temptation to remember the words of Psalm 1:

> *Blessed is the man*
> *Who walks not in the counsel of the ungodly,*
> *Nor stands in the path of sinners,*
> *Nor sits in the seat of the scornful;*

---

8 Matthew 6:13
9 Galatians 1:4
10 Psalm 34:15, 17
11 Psalm 121:7
12 Hebrews 4:12
13 Psalm 119:9, 11

But his delight is in the law of the LORD,
And in His law he meditates day and night.

In these situations it is usually easy to see which way the ungodly and sinful man would try to lead you, and then resolve to walk the other way!

So, when temptation floods our minds, we need to climb into the Word of God and let it be our protection. If you've got a Bible with you, that makes it easy. It's not so easy when you're on your own with nothing at hand. That's why it helps so much to memorize it. Not only do you have it ready in time of need, but the Holy Spirit can bring it to your mind, too.

Sing Praises

Music is interesting. It seems to affect us in ways that are not entirely obvious. Melanie has found that when she feels depressed, singing really helps. She picks up a hymnal, just opens it, and sings the first five songs she knows, all the verses. By the time she's done, often her spirit has lifted and she feels better.

Similarly, we see in 1 Samuel, that when Saul was in distress, David's music helped him:

> *And so it was, whenever the spirit from God was upon Saul, that David would take a harp and play it with his hand. Then Saul would become refreshed and well, and the distressing spirit would depart from him.*[14]

Singing God's praises, whether out loud or quietly to yourself, can lift your mind out of the gutter it's in. When going into battle, it's good to remember Martin Luther's hymn from Psalm 46:

> *A mighty fortress is our God, a bulwark never failing,*
> *Our helper, He, amid the flood of mortal ills prevailing;*
> *For still our ancient foe, Doth seek to work us woe,*
> *His craft and pow'r are great, And armed with cruel hate,*
> *On earth is not his equal.*
>
> *Did we in our own strength confide, our striving would be losing,*
> *Were not the right Man on our side, the Man of God's own choosing.*
> *Dost ask Who that may be? Christ Jesus, it is He!*

---

14 I Samuel 16:23

Lord Sabaoth, His name, From age to age the same,
And He must win the battle![15]

Or Isaac Watts' setting of Psalm 90:

O God, our help in ages past,
Our hope for years to come,
Our shelter from the stormy blast
And our eternal home

Under the shadow of Thy throne
Still may we dwell secure;
Sufficient is Thine arm alone,
And our defense is sure.[16]

Think of encouraging hymns from your own tradition or seek out new ones to suit; keep some in mind for times of trial.

> "But I will sing of Your power: Yes, I will sing aloud of Your mercy in the morning; For You have been my defense And refuge in the day of my trouble."[17]

Go to Your Authority

God has given us counselors and guides throughout our lives—parents, pastors and elders, and others who have authority in our lives. Which of these do you trust? Which can be a comfort and encouragement (and challenge) when we are falling over our own sinful feet?

Each of us has a responsibility for our own soul's health; we make decisions every moment whether we follow God's ways or our own. But God doesn't leave us without help in this world. Whether it is our family, the leaders of our church, a fellow believer we've asked to provide accountability, or one day our wife, He has given us others who can speak the truth into our lives when we are under the gun and most distracted. Let's build relationships of trust with those who are closest to our personal battlefields—and don't hesitate to call on them for prayer, counseling, and direction.

---

15 "A Mighty Fortress is Our God," by Martin Luther
16 "O God, Our Help In Ages Past," by Isaac Watts
17 Psalm 59:16

This doesn't have to be embarrassing or detailed. Just say, "I'm struggling with my thought life. Could you pray for me?" A wise counselor will do just that, then ask, "How can I help you? Is there anything you can change to make this fight easier?" That's the kind of help you need—get it.

The Five Point Defense

So in summary, the Five Point Defense is simply this:

1. **Leave or change the situation**

2. **Pray**

3. **Read Scripture**

4. **Sing to the Lord**

5. **Go to your authorities**

Usually when we teach our young sons this program, we count off each point with a finger, then fold the fingers to make "a fist to knock away temptation."

Get Accountability

It's good to have some support in your fight for purity. One useful relationship to have is an accountability partner. This might be a parent, pastor, or some other trustworthy, mature believer, that agrees to check in with you on a regular basis and ask pointed questions to keep you on track. As *iron sharpens iron,* says the proverb, *so a man sharpens the countenance of his friend.*[18] Having a comrade in this fight is a great challenge and encouragement: *Two are better than one, Because they have a good reward for their labor. For if they fall, one will lift up his companion. But woe to him who is alone when he falls, For he has no one to help him up.*[19]

Your parents may not realize how prevalent sexual temptation is these days thanks to the internet, and they may not understand how early your sexual feelings develop. You may need to say, "Hey, let's watch something else," when

---

18 Proverbs 27:17
19 Ecclesiastes 4:9-10

a certain program comes on the screen, or volunteer, "I need you to pray for me. I'm struggling with my thought life."

We were talking about this with one father just this week. At the start of the conversation, he and his wife were pretty sure that this couldn't be a problem for their thirteen-year-old son. Later on, though, the dad interrupted the discussion and said, "You know, I've been thinking back through my struggles as a teen and I realize I've done my son a disservice. I need to be talking to him about these things." Parents don't mean to leave their sons without help and counsel. It's just that they likely dealt with these issues later, and too often we parents believe that if we can just protect our children from the world, they won't be tempted to sin. It's easy to forget that sin comes from within our hearts.

Many Christian parents have made the commitment to raise their children in the church, sending them to a church-sponsored school or perhaps even homeschooling them in order to disciple them and protect them from the world. Because of that, they tend to think the temptations will be less for their children than they were for themselves. In a sense that may be true, but it often doesn't take into account how much the world has changed and how much more available sinful media is. A simple internet search can yield harrowing temptation.

So, how do you talk to your parents? *Should* you talk to your parents? It can be easy to think it's just as well *not* to tell them what's going on, especially if you have already moved out of their home. We all want our mom and dad to think well of us, and it can feel like we're about to say, "Hello, I'm here to destroy your illusions about me." Not fun.

You need to remember, though, that until you are married, there is unlikely to be anyone who is more on your side than your parents. If they are Christians, then their encouragement, counsel, support, prayer, and accountability is invaluable in your fight.

Your brothers in Christ can help you out, too. Several years ago we were involved with starting a small church in our town. The men in the church met in a private room of a local restaurant every Tuesday morning for breakfast and Bible study. Part of that time was reserved to do a quick checkup for each other. There was a list of about six questions which we knew we'd be asked every Tuesday—for example, had we been consistent in our personal devotions, did we show love to our wives and children this week, and did we keep our feet and eyes from straying after pornography or even just inappropriate entertainment. The knowledge that our closest friends in the church would ask us that question was a powerful motivator to stop, think, and turn away whenever we were tempted!

Software Tools

Another useful tool in the fight against online temptation is accountability software. Many families have used filtering and blocking programs to restrict access to immoral websites. These are particularly useful for homes where young children may be allowed on the computers, but young adults are often adept at bypassing the filters. In our home, we tried this approach but found it was too restrictive. Melanie is a lactation consultant and counsels new mothers with breastfeeding problems; she found that whenever she opened a search engine and typed "b-r-e-a-s-t", the filter would shut down her connection! In order to minister to these mothers, we found our filters turned off as much as they were on—obviously not a useful situation.

Accountability software is different. The program inserts itself between the browser and the internet, but instead of blocking websites, it simply keeps records. Once a week, the software will generate a report which is emailed to your accountability partner. It doesn't prevent you from accessing sites you shouldn't, but it keeps track of which sites you visited, the time you clicked on the link, how long you spent there, and whether it's a site that should be a concern.

If it doesn't prevent you from visiting a porn site, how does it help? Simply this—before you click on the enticing link, you remember that Thursday morning, somebody will know you went there. If he's doing his job, by Thursday evening somebody will be asking you why you did it. In other words, it takes away the false hope of secrecy, and by doing that, trains you to think before you click. Of course, God always knows, but we get pretty good at ignoring His voice; the wicked man says in his heart, *God has forgotten; He hides His face; He will never see.*[20] A face to face meeting with your pastor or father has an immediacy that is hard to match. If you are married, you might even send the report to your wife—that's what we set up in our home.

---

20 Psalm 10:11

We use a package called Covenant Eyes (named after Job's comment in Job 31:1), and we had a chance to meet with several of their developers. They explained that the software is not a *solution*—it won't prevent you from sin if that's your aim—but it is a tool which can be a very helpful part of the accountability relationship. That relationship will help us keep our paths straight, even when we leave the protection of home and childhood. "We're preparing young people for a world without filters," they concluded.[21] The goal is to help you to realize that there really is no such thing as secrecy; that someone will know. Hopefully, you will eventually always remember that Someone, your Father in heaven, will know. A real relationship with Him is the best protection of all.

We do understand that there are ways and means to defeat accountability software. If you are determined to sin, nothing can stop you. You have everything you need to rebel against God right there in your own heart and mind. You have to make it your goal to flee immorality, to pursue holiness. That means you might have to lock your phone down so you can't bypass the software. That's pretty annoying, but what's the alternative? Just like you don't leave bottles of wine in the house of an alcoholic, it's foolish to make unaccountable internet available when we know we're tempted by it. So you deal with it.

Ultimately, a young man (or an old man) keeps his heart pure by repenting of his sin, believing in Christ, and conforming himself to the image of Christ. It's a battle, we know that, but it's very worth it. One day your bride will thank you. Even better than that, one day the Lord may say to you, "Well done, *good and faithful servant.*"[22]

---

21 You can get more information about this program at www.RaisingRealMen.com/safety. If you wish to try it for a month free, either use that link or enter the discount code 'raisingrealmen.' Either way, you will also support our ministry.

22 Matthew 25:21

Summary

- **Deal with immediate temptation with the Five Point Defense**

    1. Leave the situation (or change it)

    2. Pray to God

    3. Read Your Bible

    4. Sing Praises

    5. Go to Your Authority for Help

- **Get accountability. Find someone who can ask you hard questions.**

- **Use software to hold you accountable.**

- **Repent, believe, and pursue holiness.**

5

Recovering From a Fall

Getting Back in the Battle

What if you have already fallen into the trap? You've developed a taste for pornography, or self-stimulation, or any of a hundred other forms of sexual sin? Is it too late to change? Too much to overcome?

It's a serious question in a world where so many young men have engaged in pornography before they've even left home. When nearly all young men have committed fornication in the heart, the battle seems one almost impossible to win—but it's not.

Once a guy had to do some pretty sketchy things to gain access to porn. He had to shoplift or search through other people's belongings. The chance of getting caught was pretty high, too.

Now, it seems like it comes looking for you. Misspell a word while surfing on the internet and wow, suddenly temptation floods your screen. Show some interest in world affairs and while you're trying to read the news, soft-core porn is in your sidebar. Give the wrong kind of girl your phone number and it gets delivered straight to your phone. It's hard to escape it.

Don't Lose Hope

Paul's letter sent into the sexualized culture of Corinth is very explicit.

Do you not know that the unrighteous will not inherit the kingdom of God? Do not be deceived. Neither fornicators, nor idolaters, nor adulterers, nor homosexuals, nor sodomites, nor thieves, nor covetous, nor drunkards, nor revilers, nor extortioners will inherit the kingdom of God.[1]

When Paul begins to list lifestyles that lead to condemnation, four of the first five are sexual, involving relations and acts which break the basic requirement of God's design—no sexual expression outside of marriage. It was rampant in Corinth, and Paul said in effect, "Don't let the culture tell you that it's all normal. It's not. It's gravely sinful, and God will close the door on people who live this way."

And such were some of you, he said. Yes, people like you. Your neighbors in the church. Yourself.

But—this is the key—*But you were washed, but you were sanctified, but you were justified in the name of the Lord Jesus and by the Spirit of our God.*[2]

That's the difference. God saved these sinners, purified them from their sin, sanctified them and made them holy, and declared them no longer guilty in His sight. Jesus *"gave Himself for us, that He might redeem us from every lawless deed and purify for Himself His own special people, zealous for good works."*[3]

So it's important to remember first that as bad as this sin is—and Scripture tells us that even looking at pornography breaks God's law just as surely as seduction and rape—as bad as it is, it's not the unpardonable sin. Paul looked squarely at the filth in Corinth and told those believers, "That's what you were, but God changed you and everything is cleared off the books. The debt has been paid." There is forgiveness available for the fallen sinner who turns away from the sin and seeks God and His righteousness.

God Already Knows About It

You have to remember too that God knows, to the last detail. When you thought you sinned in secret, God was a present witness; in fact, He already

---

1 1 Corinthians 6:9-10
2 1 Corinthians 6:11
3 Titus 2:14

had plans in place to deal with your sin and make it to serve His own purposes. You have nothing which can be hidden from His sight and knowledge, so God was neither surprised nor shocked at your fall. There's nothing to keep back from Him now.

How Do You Start Back on God's Road?

The apostle John wrote, *If we say that we have no sin, we deceive ourselves, and the truth is not in us. If we confess our sins, He is faithful and just to forgive us our sins and to cleanse us from all unrighteousness.*[4] David, writing in the Psalms, said,

> *Blessed* is he whose *transgression* is *forgiven,* Whose *sin* is *covered. Blessed* is *the man to whom the* LORD *does not impute iniquity, And in whose spirit* there is *no deceit. … I acknowledged my sin to You, And my iniquity I have not hidden. I said, 'I will confess my transgressions to the* LORD,' *And You forgave the iniquity of my sin.*[5]

You have to honestly admit to yourself and God that you have broken His commandments, violated His will, and given yourself over to immorality. God offers forgiveness and cleansing from these sins, but it comes at a cost—you can never forget that an innocent Man voluntarily took the punishment for the sins of the people God forgives.

And you can't take that cleansing and leap right back into the sewer. Jesus once forgave a woman who was caught in the very act of adultery, but His last word to her was both a release and a command—*"Go and sin no more."*[6] Your blood-bought pardon is not a reset button to allow you to start over in your sin, like a dog returning to its vomit. *He who covers his sins will not prosper,* the Scripture says, *But whoever confesses and forsakes* them *will have mercy.*[7] This is what the Bible calls repentance—a change of mind and direction.

As you get back on the road to follow God's will, you'll find it's hard going. Jesus invites His followers to imitate Him: *"Take My yoke upon you and learn from Me, for I am gentle and lowly in heart, and you will find rest for your souls. For My yoke is easy and My burden is light."*[8] He will give us the strength and the

4 1 John 1:8-9
5 Psalm 32:1-2, 5
6 John 8:11
7 Proverbs 28:13 (emphasis added)
8 Matthew 11:29-30

will to follow Him—yet He also warns that His road is challenging. *"Enter by the narrow gate ... Because narrow is the gate and difficult is the way which leads to life, and there are few who find it."* [9]

Prepare for a Fight

That's true in *normal* circumstances. With sexual immorality, particularly pornography, you are dealing with addictive behaviors. The physical changes in your brain and hormones in response to the sin make it difficult to break free—it's more than a habit. And your enemy hates to lose a captive. If he can throw more temptation your way and pull you back into his orbits, he'll do it.

Recognize too that if Satan can't destroy you, he'll do his best to defeat you. When the hook is baited and offered to the intended prey, his siren call is "No one will ever know ... It's perfectly normal ... It's just looking ... Not even real people ... A little bit won't hurt ..." You probably recognize the line.

But when the bait is taken, he sets the hook, and *hard.* Now his narrative changes to mocking and condemnation. "Ho, I've got you now! What a slimeball! What a loser! And you call yourself a *believer*—what a hypocrite *you* are! And what will people think? What will your *mother* say? What will your *pastor* think? Boy, are you cooked ... you might as well give up." If he can't claim you as his own, he'll do his best to break your courage to serve in God's army against him.

And this is where you have to fall on God's mercy and the promises of His word. Remember Paul's encouragement to the Corinthians—*And such were some of you. But you were washed, but you were sanctified, but you were justified ...* [10] If God has forgiven you, He's purged your record. He knew the full depth of your depravity and He still put it aside for the sake of Jesus. *If You, O Lord, should mark iniquities, O Lord, who could stand?* asks the Psalmist. *But there is forgiveness with You, That You may be feared.* [11]

Better yet, There is *therefore now no condemnation to those who are in Christ Jesus, who do not walk according to the flesh, but according to the Spirit. For the law of the Spirit of life in Christ Jesus has made me free from the law of sin and death,*

9 Matthew 7:13-14
10 1 Corinthians 6:11
11 Psalm 130:3-4

wrote the apostle Paul, this time to the church in Rome. *If God is for us, who can be against us?* [12]

Ultimately, the essential part of recovering is to repent of our sin and trust in Jesus, understanding that He took the punishment for all of our sin on the cross. Then we are truly forgiven and can begin to live a life that is pleasing to God.

But know that the road will take time.

Breaking the Chains

One of the obstacles you'll need to overcome in this battle for purity is a physical one. Internet porn and masturbation are physically addictive.

When you are exposed to sexual things, your brain produces dopamine, a kind of reward, or feel-good, hormone among several others. This is a provision of God to bless your marriage, to remind you to be intimate with your wife. However, when you are exposed to more stimulation than is normal for a marital relationship, such as when you flip between windows in your browser consuming porn, or when you add in the excitement of the forbidden, your brain may produce way too much dopamine. In response to this overload, the receptors for the hormone in your brain may become less sensitive. You may see where this is going. The next time, you are tempted to watch more or worse to get the same thrill. Lust is never satisfied. [13]

This has a host of effects. Doctors have noticed a huge growth in the number of young men coming in who have discovered after indulging for some time in porn use, they can't respond to a woman normally. They are impotent to all but porn. Tragically, we've read stories of young men who married thinking that would cure their porn habit, only to find out on their wedding night that they had to sneak into the bathroom and watch porn on their phone to become aroused. Can you imagine the pain and damage that does their lovely brides? Really! That scenario reeks of shame and failure, but that's where this stuff is headed, guys.

---

12 Romans 8:1-2, 31

13 Black, Sam. The Porn Circuit: Understand Your Brain and Break Porn Habits in 90 Days. Covenant Eyes, 2013.

The problem is that this pleasure hormone release is just exactly what is happening in substance abuse. Your brain also begins to form a bond, attachment, or habit to seek pleasure in that way. These hormones are meant to bond you to your wife; instead they are bonding you to sin. The substance or activity, the sin, gives the brain pleasure and the brain craves more of it. Drives you to seek more of it. Sees opportunities everywhere. Becomes obsessed and addicted.

Don't believe it? Ask yourself these two questions:

• **Can you go thirty days without watching porn or masturbating? If you aren't addicted, it shouldn't be a problem, right?**

• **Are you tempted to watch porn or masturbate when you are depressed or under stress? Does it change your mood?**[14]

If it's mood-altering and you can't stop, what you have is an addiction. What do you do now?

Well, you've got to break it. Right now that may seem impossible, but it isn't!

I can do all things through Christ who strengthens me.[15]

If you've trusted Christ to save you, this sin is done for, paid for, cancelled. You've got to get out of those graveclothes and start living like a new creation. After all, He came to *set at liberty those who are oppressed.* [16]

Set a Goal

The good news is that your brain can recover! You can restore your hormone receptors to normal, get rid of those sinful ruts of behavior, and reset your thinking. The bad news is that you are looking at three to six months or more of complete abstinence to get there. Set some initial goals: Can I make it 24 hours? Three days? A week? Two weeks? Every time you resist temptation, you get a little stronger spiritually and the connection to sin in your brain gets a little weaker.

---

14 Black, p4. Questions suggested by Dr. Mark Laaser, as quoted in Black.
15 Philippians 4:13
16 Isaiah 61:1 and Luke 4:18

Make a Plan

Blogger and author Tim Challies gives us great advice when he says, "When you are at your best, plan for when you are at your worst."[17] Now's the time to get a game plan going.

What are your triggers? What makes you want to sin in this way? We don't mean the visual images or fantasies, but what situations make you vulnerable? Do you remember the Five Point Defense we talked about in the chapter about fighting temptation? This takes the first point, Leave or Change the Situation, and makes it offensive, not just defensive. Are you tempted late at night? Maybe you need to stay up later until you are really sleepy, or go to bed earlier before you get too tired. Maybe you need to put your phone in your car before you go to bed, or get a godly roommate to share your room with. If you are tempted in the shower, make a game of finding out how fast you can shower and get dressed. Reward yourself if you beat your previous time. Find a way to avoid those situations that make you more vulnerable.

If you are in a relationship that has veered into sexual sin, you're going to have to put some strict limits on yourselves. You can't commit those sins if you aren't ever alone together. You can still have private talks, but choose public places to have those talks. That may seem awkward, but if it keeps you out of sin, it will be better for both of you. Explain to her your commitment to purity and your realization that you have not protected her and honored her as you should have. When you do sexual things with a girl you aren't married to (and we mean anything beyond holding hands or a simple hug or perhaps kiss in the later stages of courtship, depending on your convictions), you are telling her that you do not value her or any child that may be conceived enough to give her the protection of your name and commitment to love and support that comes with marriage. It's a trust issue. If she can't trust you to do what's best for her (and sexual sin clearly isn't) when you are trying to win her, how can she trust you to love her sacrificially after marriage? Well, really, she can't. Instead, tell her you are incredibly attracted to her (so she doesn't feel you have lost interest), so you have to be strict with yourself to do what's right. If she tries to undermine that, you probably need to let that relationship go. A Christ-centered relationship will draw you both closer to Him, not lead you into sin.

---

17 Challies, Tim. "When You're at Your Best, Plan for Your Worst." www.challies.com/christian-living/when-youre-at-your-best-plan-for-your-worst

Like we talked about earlier, in the chapter on fighting temptation, you have to avoid error-likely situations. You are more likely to succumb to temptation when you are tired, sick, under the influence of alcohol or drugs, alone, in the dark…you get the picture. Weaken your judgment or make sin easier and of course, it's easier to sin. Avoid those situations assiduously and you're less likely to commit the errors.

Get In The Battle

You are breaking an addiction just like a drunkard who goes on the wagon, so sometimes your body will give you a difficult time. Recognize you might have trouble sleeping, if you've been masturbating at night. You might feel depressed and moody. That's normal. If it's difficult to bear, you may need to get some help.[18] Remember that these things will pass! You are helping your brain and body out of a state that tempts you to sin and separate yourself from God. It's worth the struggle.

So, don't be alarmed if you have some physical, emotional, or mental struggles, too. You might feel distracted at school or work, your hands might shake, you might just feel awful. This is a sign that you have (had) a problem and you are getting rid of it! Rejoice to see those signs that you are getting this out of your system, if you are dealing with this.

Just like a general examines the battlefield and looks for any vulnerability in his line, you're going to need to deal with the things that are open doors to temptation for you. For many guys, this means you need to do something to protect yourself when you are on the computer or tablet or your phone or gaming device. First, get rid of **anything** on there that tempts you to sin, even if it's innocent-looking at first glance. Remember, you want to be done with hiding sin. Of course, deleting it from your hard drive doesn't mean it can't be recovered by someone someday. The only way to do that is to destroy the hard drive. If you have been downloading the really perverted stuff, some of which is illegal, you might want to consider that. Replacing a hard drive is a small price to pay for avoiding a felony conviction.

---

18 We've found that sometimes fish oil, vitamin D, and probiotics may help alleviate feelings of depression. If they don't help, St. John's Wort or L-methylfolate may, or you may want to talk to a Christian counselor or physician if your depression is severe. If you have having thoughts of hurting yourself, immediately seek help—right now, today.

We read of a Christian husband and father who began looking at internet porn. Those sites try to draw you into more perverse habits because that's what they can charge money for. Before long, he was looking at pictures of underage girls. Finally the horror of what he was doing hit him and he repented. He confessed to his wife and pastor, deleted the evil files he'd downloaded, and installed accountability software on all his devices. He broke the addiction. Sometime later, though, there was a knock on the door. It was law enforcement, who had traced his IP address as accessing an illegal site. They presented a search warrant and took his computers into custody. They were able to recover the files and he went to prison. Some kinds of porn can cost you your freedom.

So, get rid of anything sinful on your devices and install accountability software on everything. Then arrange to send your reports to someone with the guts to call you on the carpet. We'll talk about that later. On devices you can get around the software, find a way to lock them down. One young man installed the accountability software's browser on his smartphone[19], deleted all other ways to get online, and installed a password that had to be entered to change anything. He had his accountability partner enter the password, the young man never even saw it. Annoying? Sure, but it worked.

Changing Your Response

Several years ago, we all got the flu, but Hal couldn't get well. Eventually he went to the doctor and a chest x-ray showed he had pneumonia—and a huge tumor behind his breastbone—one of the only places on his body he could have had a tumor that size and not known it. Soon we found out he had stage IV cancer. That's end stage, as bad as it gets. We're best friends. We've been best friends from the beginning, before we even married, and this hit Melanie like a truck. She didn't want to break down in front of Hal, so she would go upstairs and lock herself in the bathroom and weep. She would wake up in the mornings, be happy a minute or two, then remember the situation and be crushed by anxiety and dread. All day, every time it came to mind, it would fall on her like an unbearable burden. She'd worry about how to raise six sons without their father, how to support such a large family by herself, and how to keep going without her best friend and husband. One day she realized that all that worry wasn't actually accomplishing anything. Actually, it was a temptation that

---

19 Many smartphones integrate seamlessly with accountability software, with others it's more challenging.

prevented her from taking care of the family's very real emotional and physical needs in the right way. She decided that every single time that crushing weight of anxiety hit her, she would cry out to God for the life of her husband or for God to take care of their needs. Want to know something? The overwhelming blasts of anxiety stopped. Not immediately, but soon. That fear and oppression were from the enemy and he had no desire to drive her to prayer.

You are experiencing strong temptation, too. Cry out for help. Every single time you think of a woman sexually, every single time the thought of mastur-bation crosses your mind, every single time you pick up your phone and are tempted to browse, pray. Pray hard. Don't let the thought even take complete form in your mind before you start praying. Pray for help to resist temptation. Pray for your future wife. Pray for your mind to be cleansed. God has promised us that He would help us,

> God is our refuge and strength,
> A very present help in trouble.[20]

Get Somebody on Your Team

S exuality is meant to be private, a special secret thing shared between husband and wife. We also too often try to hide our sin. Put the two together and your stomach shrivels up into a little hard knot when we say, get somebody to help you. We know. Still, you need to do it. The Word says,

> Whoever conceals his transgressions will not prosper, but he who confesses and forsakes them will obtain mercy.[21]

This is a tough sin to beat, and it's important that you beat it. Sexual sin will affect your marriage, your relationship to God, and a whole host of other issues in your life. You need all the help you can get.

It's difficult to know who to confide in, though. We would suggest, even if you are an adult, that you start with your father (or your mother). They love you more than anyone else and they want to see you happy and successful. Of course, if your parents aren't Christians, they may not understand what the big deal is. Even if they are, they may not be helpful for one reason or another.

---

20 Psalm 46:1
21 Proverbs 28:13 ESV

Perhaps they're fighting their own battles and don't feel able to help you, or they may be too embarrassed to give you much help. Do try, though, if they are believers. You may be surprised how well they handle it and how much they can help you with prayer, advice, and love. Give them the chance.

The next place to look is in the leadership of your church. God has given those men to watch over us and help us. Take advantage of that. Choose the one you have the most connection with and ask for his help in beating this. We suspect he'll be glad to help.

Derrick was a married man with children. A man who loved God, his wife, his family, and his country. He'd made a career out of the military. A few years ago, he was mobilized to the Middle East. His unit there was just steeped in sexual sin. Watching porn was rampant, even acting out sin that was strictly forbidden by regulations was common. Derrick was lonely and stressed (error-likely situation) and before long he was addicted to porn like he had been as an unsaved teen.

When he came back home, he couldn't hide it long. When his wife found out, she was just devastated. She felt ugly and unwanted, though she wasn't. She felt like a failure, like she couldn't meet her husband's needs, which wasn't true. He had a sin issue, not an unmet need. When Derrick saw his dear bride so hurt, he repented. It didn't last long, though. Before long, he was stopping on the way home to feed his habit.

With his marriage at stake, Derrick went to the elders of his church, desperate. He asked them to hold him to the line. He installed an app on his phone that would notify them if he strayed from a predetermined path between work and home. It sounds extreme, but it's what he needed to break his slavery to the sin and to restore his marriage.

Maybe all you need is someone to receive your accountability reports and to look you in the eye and ask how it's going. Maybe that doesn't seem like much, but it can be the guardrail that holds you back from the cliff when you are feeling weak.

The world acts like this kind of sin is no big deal. At least, it used to. That's changing. We've read about tens of thousands of young men who aren't even Christians trying to kick this habit because it's messing them up, it's dominating their lives. In a world where so many fall, can you stand? Can you stand back up if you've fallen? Absolutely.

Jesus said *"I have not come to call the righteous, but sinners, to repentance."*[22]

Here's the promise:

> *If we confess our sins, He is faithful and just to forgive us our sins and to cleanse us from all unrighteousness.*[23]

That's the goal. Because all this fight isn't just against something, it's for something. It's for your Savior and it's for your bride. We'll be talking about that next.

---

22 Luke 5:32 ESV
23 1 John 1:9 ESV

Summary

- Don't be discouraged, there's a way out.

- This is why Jesus died! Repent, believe, be restored.

- It's not going to be easy to get rid of this sin, but it's worth it.

- Sometimes there are physical, emotional or mental obstacles, but they will go away.

- You'll need to set goals.

- You'll need to avoid error-likely situations.

- You need to get help with accountability.

- You can be cleansed, made whole, be made right with God.

6

GUYS AND GIRLS

Aiming For the Prize

It was an afternoon wedding, and my friends and I were changing into our tuxedos in the church nursery. Things went quickly, and we had time on our hands before we were due in the sanctuary. One of the men suggested we sing a few hymns, and ducked into the auditorium for an armload of songbooks.

One of the requests was the old German hymn, "Praise to the Lord, the Almighty." All of us loved to sing, and as the harmonies rolled out, I was struck by the third verse. It talks about God's absolute kingship over all of Creation, and His particular care for His people.

Hast thou not seen, asked the hymn writer,
How thy desires e'er have been
Granted in what He ordaineth?

Wow, was I ever there. After years of friendship, deepening into love, I was about to marry the girl I most desired. This was God's blessing, and I could sing with all my heart—yes indeed, this was God's special plan for me, and He had brought it to pass!

And a half hour later, standing at the front of the church, I glimpsed my bride as she stepped into view at the far end of the aisle. My heart leaped and I felt my face split in a totally uncontrollable grin. There was no fear, no shame, no doubt, only a pure surging joy like sunlight. I didn't have to define beauty for myself—she was walking down the aisle, and she was God's gift to *me*. It was almost too much to stand... but I didn't want to miss a moment of it!

Now, thirty years later, I can look back and say—I didn't know the half of it, how good marriage was going to be. – Hal

So, how do you get from here (i.e., single) to there (i.e., married)? And how do you get there in a godly way? Marriage is for life and the path you take to the altar will affect the rest of your days on earth. So, let's talk about it.

Relationships

The first thing to consider is the relationship between you and *all* the women in your life. What should that be?

The Word of God makes it plain, when Paul tells young Timothy to treat ... *older women as mothers, younger women as sisters, with all purity.*[1]

That doesn't leave any room at all for sexuality outside marriage, does it? And as we've discussed in previous chapters, there are pages and pages of warnings not to go down that path of sex before marriage or sex outside of marriage.

On the other hand, this passage does *not* tell us to treat women like strangers, with suspicion and alarm. Timothy was a young man, and young enough that people might not take him seriously as a missionary pastor; we know this because Paul had to encourage him, *"Let no one despise your youth ..."*[2] So when Paul speaks of "younger women" he's probably thinking of Timothy's peer group. If he wasn't married yet, these would be the most likely women he'd consider. And Paul says treat them like sisters.

How do you treat your sister? With honor, definitely, but also with friendly regard and warmth. There should not be stiffness and formality, a stand-offish, arms-length, I-might-get-cooties attitude. You just interact naturally as people who have some things in common.

---

1 1 Timothy 5:2
2 1 Timothy 4:12. The NASB says, "Let no one look down on your youthfulness ..."

The Value and Wisdom of Friendship

Just like the church in Corinth, many in the modern conservative church movement have looked at the culture around us and shudder in horror. They ask the question, "With so much temptation around, with the moral ground slippery underfoot, is it even *safe* to interact with the opposite sex? Is it even *possible* to have an innocent relationship, outside of your own family?"

Some of our friends have said emphatically, "No!" In their view, platonic friendships between men and women are simply impossible. But really? Is this the life of siblings, like Paul suggested? No, it's not. Within your family, you and your sister spend time talking, working together, and enjoying the innocent pleasures of life – just the same as you would with your brother! Does dinner with your family leave you boiling with lust? Of course not. Well, then …

We would say that if these activities can be done with your sister "*with all purity*," as Paul enjoined, then they are probably okay to do with the young women in your life. That means no sexual stuff at all, but you shouldn't close the door on casual interaction and fellowship.

In fact, we think you *ought* to make friends with the girls you know, especially in the years approaching the time you'll be looking for a wife. What do friends do? They talk about current events, discuss politics, review books and movies. They might share what they're learning from God's word. They enjoy interests and hobbies together. They get to know one another.

But a *sister*-sister is different than a church sister, you might say, and a young woman you might be attracted to is altogether different again. To some extent, we'd agree. Sitting around in your pajamas opening Christmas presents? Okay with your sibling, not cool with the girl from Bible study. We get that. But what concerns us is advice we hear that unmarried girls and guys should never be talking one-on-one—not even at a crowded hamburger stand, or over a cup of coffee at the doughnut store. There's no reason we see that Christian young people can't talk to one another in public situations without harming someone's morals or reputation.

We do have a couple of cautions, though. A Christian man with honorable intent doesn't want to send the wrong message to a young woman, or do anything which might be *received* as the wrong message whether he intended it or not. He shouldn't behave or speak in a manner that suggests more interest than he actually has.

This goes both ways, of course. A young woman might choose a pretty outfit for a summer afternoon and not realize that what just looks cute to her eye, might be seen as "flirtatious" by a young man—a message she did *not* intend to send. Guys are easily distracted by a girl's figure.

Likewise, girls can be distracted by a guy's attention. You may have a passion for a particular issue. Maybe it's spiritual, maybe it's political, maybe it's something else. You can talk for hours, with great devotion, about your favorite topic. Fine—but realize that if you share that conversation with a girl one-on-one, she can easily mistake, "He's passionate about wildlife," for, "He's sharing his heart! He's passionate about *me!*"

That's one reason it's a good idea to have *several* female friends, and be careful not to focus your attention exclusively on one until you're ready to start looking for a potential mate (which we'll talk about in a minute). That singular attention could be misunderstood, and you need to avoid leading a girl toward a romantic interest if you don't have one or it's not an appropriate time yet.

On the other hand, if it's getting to that time in your life and you think there's potential in a frienship, don't *deny* interest too quickly.

A young man told us he'd been meeting a young woman for lunch. They worked for different organizations but had some interests in common, and while he still thought of her as a good friend, he was praying and considering whether they should be more, one day. On the way out of the office one day, a co-worker asked her, "So, is this your boyfriend?" The young man was caught flat-footed, and in his embarrassment he blurted, "Oh, no! We're just friends!" After all, he hadn't really expressed interest to *her* yet and this didn't seem the time.

However, his female friend heard a message he hadn't intended. A couple of weeks later she had begun a relationship with another guy, and eventually they were married.

Our friend would have done better to keep his mouth shut and let the young woman answer. Perhaps he could have smiled broadly and kept walking, or he could have said something ambiguous like, "We'll see," perhaps with a raised eyebrow. In our house, we jokingly refer to this as "Rule Six" – If the girl of your dreams suddenly falls into your arms, don't drop her! Don't be too quick to deny interest that's there.

Another caution concerns the books and speakers making the rounds discouraging boy-girl friendship. One, in fact, likens it to *impurity*. We strongly disagree. Friendship is not forbidden in Scripture, and we do not have the option of declaring things to be sin that are not condemned as such in the Word of God. These speakers and authors imply that by treating these platonic relationships as sinful – or nearly so — that you'll protect yourself from falling into undeniable sin. However, this is the source of the Pharisees' error—creating extra-Biblical rules in hope of fencing off the undoubted sin. Eventually, their man-made rules carried the weight of Scripture for their followers. Jesus spoke against them, saying *"they bind heavy burdens, hard to bear, and lay* them *on men's shoulders; but they* themselves *will not move them with one of their fingers."*[3]

This became all too evident recently when one of these very speakers was exposed for having inappropriate relationships with young women under his authority—all while teaching others to avoid even innocent friendships. That's just the kind of hypocrisy the Lord was talking about here.

Now, one teacher's hypocrisy doesn't automatically negate everything he was teaching, but in this case, it's clear the requirements he taught for relationships between single adults went far beyond Scripture.

So, what do you do if you'd like to be friends with a young woman, but find she doesn't believe in friendships between guys and girls? You have a few options:

- **You can shrug your shoulders, move on, and look for someone more open to friendship.**

- **You can explain your friendly intentions to her if she will allow it.**

- **You can go to her dad and explain that you would like to get to know her as a friend, that you don't intend to try and win her heart at this time, and you will treat her honorably.**

The last option may be the most difficult, but it may be worth a try. At the very least, you will get an opportunity to get to know her father and find

---

3 Matthew 23:4

out if he's a good man with his daughter's best interest at heart, or if he's an overcontrolling and unreasonable dad. In that case, it may be best to leave this family alone!

"Just" Friends

So what kind of things can you do with a friend who is a girl, but not a girl-friend? What will help you get to know each other better?

The easiest and most obvious is to do profitable things with groups of friends:

- **Go to a movie with several friends and discuss it afterward over coffee**

- **Take a group to a contra dance, English country dance, or a square dance (they're great fun, and less couple-oriented than some other dancing)**

- **Organize a hymn sing**

- **Volunteer to help out with a charity or at an elderly widow's house**

- **Take a hike or a canoe trip**

These kinds of activities will let you get to know somebody in a low-stress way, and they don't imply more attachment or commitment than appropriate.

At the same time, don't make life changing decisions solely on the basis of group acquaintance. Recently we dealt with this question on our *Raising Real Men* blog:

> We have friends who make this argument [for meetings in groups-only, until the point of engagement]. We'd reply that you can learn a lot about a person from group interaction, but it will only be things the person wants to make public within that group. Maybe they have views that aren't in style for that group (are groups of young people ever foolish, opinionated, unkind, or unbiblical?) Or frankly, maybe they're hiding a rebellious attitude that they don't want their parents to know yet, and conforming to the group's expectations to stay under cover. We expect most friendships to operate in that public space, especially for

our younger children, but before a relationship gains a formal status, there really needs to be some private conversation. And we have to recognize, too, that as our children grow older, it becomes more and more difficult to organize those group activities because of work and student schedules; it's much easier to get a group of teenagers together than a gathering of twenty-somethings.[4]

Beginning to Focus

The day may come that you want to spend more time with your friend. Perhaps you find you enjoy her company a great deal, or maybe you are wondering if she is someone you want to consider for marriage one day. What then?

A good start is to just step aside and talk at church. Or go for a walk after church. Or meet for coffee or ice cream. Find an errand to do together. One-on-one time doesn't need to be a formal date, and most of the time, it won't be—nor should it be.

Better yet, work on a project together. Perhaps you can help organize a church event together, or plan a fellowship for your friends, or work on a charitable project, or help either of your families with a job they need done. Working together reveals a lot about a person: Are they diligent or lazy? Are they determined or do they give up easily? How do they deal with exasperation or discomfort? What are they like when they're tired? When you work at an awful job together and enjoy it because the other person is there, that's a good sign.

Early in this time, you need to find out what she thinks about Christ. Is she a real believer? Does our friendship draw me closer to the Lord or draw me away from Him? Does she seem to be growing in grace and spiritual matters? faith and the same you do.

After the spiritual concerns, ask her opinion of a hundred different things – politics, the world, ministry, books and movies, and more.

Just be careful not to speak specifically of a possible future like marriage to each other or children you might have together. The early

4 Young, Hal and Melanie. "Dating and Courtship: It's Just Coffee." *Raising Real Men* blog, August 18, 2014. http://www.raisingrealmen.com/2014/08/courtship-its-just-coffee/

stages of this relationship should focus on "Tell me about yourself," not, "What will our future together look like?" Those sort of "someday" discussions can flutter a girl's mind if it's not the right time. If she brings them up, you should certainly take note of anything she says about them—but you shouldn't introduce those topics yourself just yet.

You also have to consider honestly whether you really enjoy each other's company. This is another reason that group activities alone are not sufficient; how many times have we felt very familiar with someone because we see them at church, in group meetings, at the gym, or around the neighborhood—yet in fact, we really know very little about them or their habits. People are kind of like dogs—some of them have an immediate rapport, while others bristle at the very sight of each other. A person can be a perfectly nice Christian and yet have a personality that clashes with your own and grates on your nerves. That's okay, but that sort of mismatched relationship is in for struggle!

Lord willing, the time will come when you begin thinking friendship with that certain girl may just not be enough. You begin thinking that it's time to figure out the Lord's will for the two of you as a couple. Should you seriously consider marriage? Up to this point, it's been a good idea to avoid romance, overt flirtation, or planning a life together. Friendship should be based on treating one another as brother and sister in Christ and building a relationship that leaves no one embarrassed or ashamed.

Here comes another controversy, though: We hear Christian leaders suggesting a wide range of paths to get from friendship to marriage. We've heard recommendations of everything from dating a variety of people (never the same one twice in a row) to betrothal plans that are practically arranged marriages—and we've read both recommendations in the same month!

Serious, conservative Christians come down on all sides of the question. What's the truth? What's the Biblical pattern? Do you ever feel like we did, ready to cry out, "Just tell me what to do, so we can do this right!"

The Biblical Way to Find a Mate

It would be easy if there were just a step-by-step method to finding the right mate in the right way. In many situations, though, God does not give us a checklist to follow, but His word and His Spirit as our guides. Sometimes those seem harder to grasp! As we wrote on our blog, **When it comes to marriage or anything else, the question for Christians should always start with "What has God told us? What does the Bible say?"**

As we've studied this matter through, we've come to a surprising conclusion: the Bible doesn't give many specific directions. This is the first thing we have to grasp –

The process of finding a mate is largely a matter of Christian liberty.

Things would be so much easier if there were clear directions and boundaries. There are, of course, when you consider commandments to consider others more highly than yourself, to avoid immorality, to keep from defrauding one another with promises and expectations that cannot or will not be met. Yet the process of dating and courtship—of intentionally seeking a mate—mostly remains in the space of regulated liberty.

There is no definitive pattern in Scripture for how we find our mates—which means we give each other grace about the patterns we choose.

If you want a Biblical pattern for finding a wife, you might send a servant to choose one from your cousins (that's what Abraham did for Isaac). You might go to a dance and kidnap one of the young ladies for yourself, and let your family smooth it over with her parents afterward (that's what happened at Shiloh). If you're a woman, you might visit your kinsman's workplace and curl up at his feet while he naps (that's what Ruth did with Boaz). Hmmmm ... No, we don't think those methods would work today. Or, you might be like the hundreds of people mentioned in the Bible without reference to how they met one another and came to be married.

Where the Scriptures are clear, we can be very clear, but where they are silent, or where they offer many examples without much commentary (as in this case), then we need to give each other liberty and grace to seek the Lord and our own consciences on the matter.[5]

You may be thinking, "Well, that's not much help." We get it. Sometimes liberty is a little alarming because we long for a checklist to make sure we're doing it right. God didn't give us a checklist in this area, but He did give us some principles.

Are You Both Biblically Qualified For Marriage?

It is a sign of the times that we even have to say this, but you know from Scripture that God intends men to marry women; you can't marry a member of your same sex, nor your dog nor your computer (as some have claimed!). You should both be single. You should both be adults and free to give or withhold consent. Is this too obvious?

Don't Be Unequally Yoked

The most important question to ask about a potential mate is whether she's a real Christian or not. We don't mean "Christian" as opposed to Muslim, Hindu, or atheist, but rather, does she have a saving faith in the Lord Jesus Christ? Do you see the fruit of the Spirit in her life? Is she interested in the things of God and involved in a church?

If you're a believer and she is not, then she's not for you.

Paul wrote to the church in Corinth,

Do not be unequally yoked together with unbelievers. For what fellowship has righteousness with lawlessness? And what communion has light with darkness? And what accord has Christ with Belial? Or what part has a believer with an unbeliever?[6]

---

5 Young, Hal and Melanie. "What in the World *is* Courtship? (not a cookie cutter approach)" *Raising Real Men* blog, November 7, 2013. http://www.raisingrealmen.com/2013/11/what-in-the-world-courtship/

6 2 Corinthians 6:14-15. Belial is a term which means a worthless person or one who has cast off the yoke of God's law, and therefore is also a name for Satan.

He told them that *"A wife is bound by the law as long as her husband lives; but if her husband dies, she is at liberty to be married to whom she wishes,* but only in the Lord." (emphasis added)[7] He recognized that a marriage between a believer and an unbeliever was a tense situation, and if the unbeliever abandoned the Christian spouse, Paul said the believer was free to let them go: *"a brother ... is not in bondage in such cases,"* he wrote, *"... [For] how do you know, O husband, whether you will save* your *wife?"*[8]

We talked in an earlier chapter about the broad way that leads to destruction and the narrow way that leads to life. Christians and unbelievers are on a different path; they are headed to different places. Now, if you attach a horse to front of the wagon and another horse to the back, what will happen? Nothing good, that's for sure. What about a horse and an ox, side by side? Slow-moving and hard to guide. *"Can two walk together, unless they are agreed?"* asked the prophet Amos.[9]

So from the clear direction and example of the New Testament, you have a plain principle: Don't practice "evangelistic dating," assuming you'll win your sweetheart over to your beliefs, but rather, seek out true, growing followers of Jesus Christ. Choose your "possibles" from the Christians you know.

Preparing for a Family

When we think of love and romance, we think of two people passionate about one another. Marriage is the rightful destination (and permanent home) for that, and marriage is the birth of a family.

The process of finding and deciding on a mate needs to be intentional. It can be fun, spontaneous at times, exciting, and romantic. However, it also needs to be thoughtful, considerate of others (and more than just *the other*), and honest. Your wife will be your life partner in the mission God calls you to, and you need to be reasonably convinced that your personalities, dreams, and beliefs align and harmonize toward that goal.

When you begin to focus in on the one best potential mate in view, when you find yourself seriously beginning to consider marriage to one particular

---

7 1 Corinthians 7:39
8 1 Corinthians 7:15-16
9 Amos 3:3

person, then you enter a process sometimes called courtship, sometimes called a serious relationship. It's a natural progression from friendship to something deeper, and it is a time to prayerfully assess whether God would direct you toward this person—or perhaps, away.

This is an important distinction to us. The time when a person has offered and promised marriage to another is engagement. The decision has been made and promises, usually verbal but promises nonetheless, have been made. It's the proper time to make public announcements about the relationship and to firm up plans for the ceremony and married life afterward.

Serious dating or courtship is not the same thing as engagement. It's the time of focused consideration, full of questions and what-ifs, so that you can evaluate one another's suitability and desirability in detail. However, a successful relationship is one which concludes with a definite answer—is this the right person for me to marry? It may lead to marriage, or it may just as successfully rule out a marriage.

For that reason, we strongly urge our own children and our young friends, to take this time seriously but withhold the publicity until the decision is made. No ring? Then no announcement. That way, if the Lord leads you apart, there is less embarrassment and pain. Also, there is less pressure to make a mismatched relationship "work" for the sake of saving face.

Timing

If all this is supposed to lead to marriage and marriage means family life, why should a young man who is nowhere near able to support a wife and family be trying to win a girl's heart? That implies a promise that he can't fulfill. The Word of God says in the Old Testament,

Prepare your work outside; get everything ready for yourself in the field, and after that build your house.[10]

If the increasing closeness and emotional attachment of this period is intended to point toward marriage, then consider this principle: Don't start shopping until you'll soon be able to close the deal. In other words, if you are not close to

---

10 Proverbs 24:27 ESV

ready to take on the responsibility of leading and providing for a wife and family, then you need to keep from building that kind of relationship. The Proverbs say,

> *Prepare your work outside,*
> *And make it ready for yourself in the field;*
> *Afterwards, then, build your house.*[11]

That's good advice. You probably ought not to be looking for a wife until you are getting pretty close to being able to support one. That's one reason we've discouraged our own sons from pursuing relationships beyond the friendship phase until they were adults working towards supporting themselves.

Honor Your Parents

The principle of honoring your parents is anchored in the Ten Commandments. *"Honor your father and your mother, that your days may be long upon the land which the LORD your God is giving you."*[12]

There are some teachers who expect adult children to remain under the command of their aging parents. Doesn't Paul say, *Children, obey your parents in the Lord, for this is right?*[13] The next verse renews the commandment, "Honor your father and your mother," *which is the first commandment with promise.*[14] And you see there is the difference between obeying and honoring; *children* are told to obey, while all people young and old are expected to *honor.* On top of being a commandment, it's practical wisdom when you're considering marriage.

How can you honor your parents? By including them. Talk through this process with them. Get their advice. Listen to their insight. Take it seriously. Keep them informed. And give them a chance to get to know the young woman you are interested in. This last point is really important, because the excitement and emotion of a growing relationship may blind you to important things to consider about your friend. Your parents not only have the wisdom of their years and experience, they are also able to be more objective than you are about your relationship.

---

11 Proverbs 24:27
12 Exodus 20:12
13 Ephesians 6:1
14 Ephesians 6:2

You might be looking at your family and thinking, "You don't know my parents. We don't have a close relationship, we don't share the same world view, and I don't think they believe the same things I do." That may be true. On the other hand, much of what goes into the decision to marry, and what goes into a successful marriage as well, is not dependent on your belief system. You don't have to be born again to have a decent marriage and learn from the experience. We've often heard excellent advice from older adults who frankly reject God's truth in their lives, yet understand human nature and people's character from observation. You can still show honor (and gain a lot of benefit) no matter what your parents believe. Assume they care about you and want you to be happy in the end, and give an ear to their advice; if you decide to take a different path than they recommend, you can still show them respect for their suggestions.

In the same way, help the girl you are pursuing give honor to her own parents. The same rules apply; remember they raised her to be a special young woman, didn't they? So give them a chance to get to know you, and show them respect. Try and honor their requests, if they express concerns. After all, they could be your future in-laws.

When do you need to talk to the girl's father? Do you have to get permission to see more of her than a chat after church? Again, there are teachers who are calling for young men to step up and state their intention before showing the first hint of interest to the girl. Actually, we don't see that in Scripture, so your conscience shouldn't be bound over it. However, when a young man begins to seriously think about a young woman as a possible wife, we think it's a good idea for him to talk to her dad, long before he gets the girl's emotions tied up.

In fact, some of the guys we know went to the father sooner, just to let him know they weren't messing around with his daughter, but wanted to get to know her better as a friend to see if they were a possibility for one another. Why? Because daddies love their girls and want them to be safe. If you keep everything out in the open and above board with her dad, you will make him feel better about the relationship, and make it more likely to gain his wholehearted approval for marriage, if the time comes. Since your birth families are a part of your own life and your children's lives, too, having her family on your side is a great way to start!

We encourage you to seek the counsel of your pastor or elders, as well, especially if your parents aren't Christians.

In All Purity

Remember that verse we talked about earlier about treating young women as sisters in all purity? The purity doesn't stop when you start thinking your sister-in-Christ may one day be your bride. In fact, you should become even more concerned about maintaining a right relationship. During this time of consideration, you want to show her that you can be a spiritual leader; you don't do that by luring her into sin just because you want to sin. That destroys your leadership. You want to show her that you can protect her; you don't do that by taking advantage of her. You want to show her that you would be a good father; you don't do that by taking a chance of conceiving a baby out of wedlock. Keeping the relationship pure is an important part of proving yourself as a potential husband.

If you decide to have sex before marriage, you are in effect saying to her, 'I care more about myself than I do you. I care more about satisfying this physical urge than I care about you being humiliated. I care more about satisfying my lust than I care about our baby being born without the protection of my name and our marriage.' You are, in essence, saying, "I do not love you," because love puts someone else's needs ahead of your own.'" That's not a good message to send to someone you want to marry.

Be aware. Sometimes even good girls may take chances because they don't understand the way you are made. A girl may wear shorts too short or a top too tight not because she is trying to entice you, but because she just thinks it looks pretty and she notices you notice her. Very likely, she has no idea what it is doing to you. Really. Her thoughts are not where yours are.

Girls can also take chances without realizing it, by being alone with you too late at night or in another potentially compromising situation. A girl who isn't trying to be seductive may not even think about those things. You can protect both of you without being insulting or implying sin on her part by just saying, "You know, let's go somewhere else. I don't want to be tempted. I want to treat you right." If the relationship has progressed far enough, you can add, "You are very attractive to me, so I want to be extra careful," with a smile.

This care will pay off in the end. If the relationship doesn't lead to marriage, then when you separate as a couple the two of you have nothing to be ashamed of and nothing to keep you from becoming friends as couples when you're both married to other people one day. If the relationship does lead to marriage, you can enter into your physical relationship without any baggage or guilt. Many long-married couples have told us that their biggest regret was getting involved sexually before marriage. Even though they would later marry, the sin they had shared caused a breach of trust that took years to heal. Trust us, it's worth the wait.

We want to say just a word about that, though. Many young men have had a bout with porn at some time in their single years. You need to repent and break free of it entirely before you marry—as soon as possible to put an end to the sin. You need to be porn free for several months before marriage at the very least. Why? Because the temptation doesn't go away with marriage. Guys think, "It's just 'til I get married," and then find they can't stop. Go back to Christ's warning about looking at women to lust for them; it's adultery in the heart, it's a sin against God, and it's a terrible way to start a marriage. Addiction to porn can also make you unable to physically respond to your wife and that's a humiliating thing for both of you. Get loose from it as soon as possible so your spirit, mind, and body can recover.

Guys also need to cleanse their mind of this stuff because it teaches them expectations of sex that are completely different than what most women want or expect. Porn frequently shows humiliation, aggression, or worse, when most women would be horrified, and rightfully so. You need to get this stuff cleaned up and your mind renewed so that you can treat your bride as she deserves.

Respect Each Other

> *Let nothing be done through selfish ambition or conceit, but in lowliness of mind let each esteem others better than himself. Let each of you look out not only for his own interests, but also for the interests of others.* [15]

We recommend you commit to being honest and forthright with each other and to treat one another the way you want to be treated. That means, among other things, that you don't suggest more in a relationship than you are sure about. It also means that if you decide the relationship shouldn't progress to marriage, that you talk it over first instead of pronouncing a verdict and walk-

---

15 Philippians 2:3-4

ing out, and that you close the relationship in as respectful and kind a way as possible.

Win Her Heart

As you become more and more interested in making a young woman your wife, you are going to have to convince her! Don't despise the traditional trappings of romance. Sometimes, serious and godly guys think all that stuff is silly and beneath them, but they couldn't be further from the truth. There's really good reason behind much of it. By giving gifts or paying the tab when you go out to dinner, you're saying "I can support you. I want to be your provider." Flowers and chocolate show you want her to have the lovely things and delicious treats she craves. It says, "I want to please you. I want to make you happy." When you remember special dates and give her cards, it says, "This relationship is important to me." Compliments reassure her that you find her attractive. Opening the door for her and walking on the street side of the sidewalk shows you want to protect her. Doing these things encourages the two of you to strive to please one another and to bond emotionally, an important part of preparing for marriage. It's a blast, too.

Be Intentional

Romance, in a Biblical context, is about finding a mate. Once you move beyond friendship into a deeper relationship, it needs to be about considering marriage. Let us tell you our story.

As we mentioned early, we were best friends in college. We lived in the same apartment building our first year and just enjoyed talking to one another. We frequently ate meals together or ran errands or walked to class. Neither of us had any thought of the other being a love interest. None. It seems funny now.

It was a shock the first time something like that hit our radar. Melanie's mother had come to visit her. Of course, Melanie introduced her to her friend, Hal. At the end of the visit, we all ran into each other at the elevator, exchanged pleasantries, then the ladies boarded the elevator as Hal continued down the hall. On the way down, Melanie's mom turned to her and said, out of the blue, "Melanie, I think that's the man you are going to marry."

Now, that's the one and only time she's ever said anything prophetic at all, and it sure didn't seem like it at the time because Melanie responded angrily, "Mama! Don't ruin this friendship!" Melanie didn't understand at the time that friendship and romance weren't mutually exclusive. She didn't share the story with Hal until we were engaged!

Our second year, Melanie transferred to another university, but we kept up our friendship. This was before email, much less smartphones or social media (yeah, we're dinosaurs); we wrote letters and talked on the phone. The next summer, Melanie was working in an urban inner city ministry and Hal was studying abroad when he sent her a letter that really shook her. He told her that he couldn't get his mind off her. He said he'd go out with a girl and think, "She's really pretty, but she's not as smart as Melanie," or "She's really smart, but she's not as pretty as Melanie," or "She's really smart and pretty, but she doesn't love the Lord like Melanie." He finally suggested they consider making their friendship more.

Melanie panicked. She really valued his friendship, wasn't interested in him *that* way, and was afraid of losing what they had. When they got back to their respective colleges, she invited him up to stay with a male friend for a football game. Over the weekend she successfully talked him out of the idea, but he talked *her* into it. She didn't say anything right then, but she couldn't get over how he had grown in the Lord! When they'd been at school together, he'd been a new believer; now he was a student leader among Christians on campus. He'd become a man she could follow.

When he got back to college he called her to say he understood about not taking the relationship any further. Melanie broke in and asked, "Are you sure?" and Hal's stomach flipped over. Suddenly everything changed. We spent the next several months as confused friends!

We finally decided to end the farce and see what the Lord did have in store for us. We'd been friends long enough and knew each other too well to start a traditional, shallow sort of dating relationship, though.

What we landed on seemed odd at the time but it suited our personalities. First, we decided to go about this in a thoughtful way: we committed to pray, both of us, together and separately, about whether the Lord would have us marry. We agreed to study the same passages of Scripture in our devotions so we could discuss what God was teaching us from our reading.

Next, we each made a list of all the things that concerned us about marriage. Those lists covered the sublime to the ridiculous! They included important things like how many children we wanted and what kind of church we wanted to attend, and less important (even silly) things like who would take out the trash or whether the toilet paper would go over the top of the roll or hang underneath. Each time we could meet together, we'd talk about a couple of the questions on the list. It didn't take very long before it became obvious to both of us that we were meant for each other. Our hearts were being knit together and we began to fall in love. The neat thing is that we did it without any fear about what it would be like to be married; we were coming to agreement on all the things we were talking about. It was such a blessing to start our marriage in so much harmony. Since then we've changed our minds on some of those things, but we started out on the same page, changed our minds together, and ended up in agreement again. That cuts out a lot of stress! So much so that our friends and adult kids suggested we make an app to help other people do that.[16]

A program of serious questioning and discussion doesn't sound very romantic, but we found the romance came very naturally as we came more and more into agreement. Sometimes Melanie had to speak up, "Hey, why don't we go somewhere nice for dinner?" or sometimes Hal would think to send flowers when Melanie was stressed in her schoolwork or job. By Christmas, we were both thinking, "Marriage!" Hal talked to his mother and asked for her blessing, then asked Melanie's mother (both of our mothers were widows) for permission to propose. When Hal proposed, in a very romantic way, Melanie joyously accepted. Then the romance really got exciting!

We've been married nearly three decades now and we're not only still best friends, but we love each other even more than we did back then. The process of growing together as we move through life has brought us closer and closer—and we have lots more fun!

Now, are we proposing that you follow our model? Not necessarily! It worked great for us, but we've also learned this: Everyone's love story is unique, just like people are. If marriage is a picture of Christ and the church, why should we be surprised that love stories are as varied as salvation stories?

16 www.morethanfriends.io

In this area we have Christian liberty, and we don't want to put rules where God has not. We shared our story so you have at least one example of how folks can apply these principles and end up happily married. Your love story probably won't look just like ours, but we'll bet it'll be just as much fun!

Summary

- Treat young women as sisters.

- Finding a mate is largely a matter of Christian liberty within some important principles.

- You should both be Biblically qualified.

- You should both be believers.

- You should keep in mind that marriage is the start of a family.

- You should honor your parents.

- You should treat each other with respect.

- You should behave "in all purity."

- Prepare for marriage morally.

- You should be intentional.

- Christian marriage is a huge blessing.

Conclusion

The Road Ahead

Many years ago, when we lived in central California, we took our Thanks-giving vacation to drive down to San Diego. We set out to camp, but when our toddler unexpectedly threw up all over our small tent, we decided to move to a motel. We called home to let family know about the change of plans.

To our surprise, they were almost desperately worried about our safety. What we discovered was that not long after we drove past the town of Coalinga, a dust storm had swept across Interstate 5 and totally blanked visibility on a highway full of holiday traffic. Over a hundred vehicles plowed into each other in the sand-filled darkness; 14 people were killed, 114 injured. One hundred and fifty miles of interstate were shut down.

Why is this relevant?

Because when we drove down that highway, it was a bright, sunny day, clear as a bell, and traffic was moving normally. If someone had asked us about driving it later, we'd have suggested they stay alert, observe the speed limits, watch out for heavy traffic—no surprises.

The driver who followed us a very short time later had encountered utter chaos—darkness, fire, death. *His* experience might have included slamming into a stopped vehicle, then feeling more cars slamming into *his*. He may have barely escaped through a window, scrambling through broken glass and smoke, hearing the cries of the injured. He would have spoken of fear, uncertainty, and dangers no one expects.

That, gentlemen, is the situation in a rapidly changing culture. Many, if not most, of your pastors, parents, counselors, and mentors drove through their teens and twenties dealing with the same temptations your grandparents faced. Between then and now, conditions deteriorated. The threats ratcheted up, it became harder to avoid accidents, and people all around you began falling into traps that didn't exist before ... and the people that went before you may have no idea of what you're facing.

Like them, you still need to remember the basics—stay alert, observe the limits, be aware of unsafe behaviors—but the intensity of the challenge is greater than many have faced... ever. Don't underestimate it.

But, don't give up, either. God is sovereign. He placed you in this moment of history and calls you to be strong. Not only that, but He promises you a way to escape temptation.

> *No temptation has overtaken you that is not common to man. God is faithful, and he will not let you be tempted beyond your ability, but with the temptation he will also provide the way of escape, that you may be able to endure it.[1]*

And when you find you've stumbled or fallen,

> *If we say that we have no sin, we deceive ourselves, and the truth is not in us. If we confess our sins, He is faithful and just to forgive us our sins, and to cleanse us from all unrighteousness.[2]*

> *And such were some of you. But you were washed, but you were sanctified, but you were justified in the name of the Lord Jesus and by the Spirit of our God.[3]*

The challenges change, but God's law—and God's love—haven't. Don't underestimate that either. The One who created this incredible life-giving, life-affirming, life-shaking system of male and female and all that follows, is the One who promised to direct and guide and protect us as we travel down this road of life ... the dust storms of culture notwithstanding.

---

1 1 Corinthians 10:13 (ESV)
2 1 John 1:8-9
3 1 Corinthians 6:11

So, stand strong. Resist temptation. Do what's right. It really is possible, with the Lord's help, to stay away from sexual sin, to have healthy relationships with girls, to marry a godly woman and have a great relationship with her and with your children. It's not just possible, it's important and it's worth it. It's worth every moment of the battle because you serve a King who laid down His life for you and He expects it of you. And also because one day you will likely find yourself a lady's knight in shining armor. Not a knight whose armor is clean and bright because he hasn't seen battle, but one who has been tried and found victorious. Embrace the battle. Be that knight!